Dear Reader:

The book you are about to read is the latest bestseller from the St. Martin's True Crime Library, the imprint *The New York Times* calls "the leader in true crime!" Each month, we offer you a fascinating account of the latest, most sensational crime that has captured the national attention. St. Martin's is the publisher of Tina Dirmann's VANISHED AT SEA, the story of a former child actor who posed as a yacht buyer in order to lure an older couple out to sea, then robbed them and threw them overboard to their deaths. John Glatt's riveting and horrifying SECRETS IN THE CELLAR shines a light on the man who shocked the world when it was revealed that he had kept his daughter locked in his hidden basement for 24 years. In the Edgar-nominated WRITTEN IN BLOOD, Diane Fanning looks at Michael Petersen, a Marine-turned-novelist found guilty of beating his wife to death and pushing her down the stairs of their home—only to reveal another similar death from his past. In the book you now hold, IN THE MIDDLE OF THE NIGHT, Brian McDonald examines a truly horrific crime that destroyed an innocent family and stunned a community.

St. Martin's True Crime Library gives you the stories behind the headlines. Our authors take you right to the scene of the crime and into the minds of the most notorious murderers to show you what really makes them tick. St. Martin's True Crime Library paperbacks are better than the most terrifying thriller, because it's all true! The next time you want a crackling good read, make sure it's got the St. Martin's True Crime Library logo on the spine—you'll be up all night!

Charles E. Spicer, Jr.,
Executive Editor, St. Martin's True Crime Library

Titles by

BRIAN MCDONALD

Safe Harbor

In the Middle of the Night

from the True Crime Library of
St. Martin's Paperbacks

IN THE MIDDLE OF THE NIGHT

BRIAN MCDONALD

St. Martin's Paperbacks

IN THE MIDDLE OF THE NIGHT

Cover photo of house © Photodisk Superstock. Cover photo of graves by Polaris Images/Gregory Mango.

For information address St. Martin's Press, 175 Fifth Avenue, New York, NY 10010.

EAN: 978-0-312-94574-9

Printed in the United States of America

St. Martin's Paperbacks edition / October 2009

St. Martin's Paperbacks are published by St. Martin's Press, 175 Fifth Avenue, New York, NY 10010.

10 9 8 7 6 5 4 3 2

For Bernie,
who sat quietly
through all of this

ACKNOWLEDGMENTS

I would like to thank the editors at St. Martin's True Crime Library, namely Charles Spicer and Yaniv Soha, for their patience, craft and suggestions. As always, I send my love and admiration to Jane Dystel, my agent, and to her talented staff.

NOTE TO READERS

As of this writing the trial for the murders in Cheshire, Connecticut, has not been held nor has anyone yet been convicted of any crime concerning that event. The information contained in the pages that follow comes from, among other sources, published court and parole documents and interviews and exclusive correspondence with Joshua Komisarjevsky.

PROLOGUE

Sorghum Mill Drive has not changed much since that rainy July morning in 2007. Life goes on. The driveways of the handsome homes still exhibit the lives of families and children. There are bicycles, basketball hoops and SUVs that proudly display college stickers on back windows, as no doubt a white Pacifica in front of 300 Sorghum Mill Drive would have displayed one from Dartmouth. The street is still just like any other in Cheshire, Connecticut—that is, until you get to the corner of Hotchkiss Ridge, where once the Petit home stood. Damaged from fire, holding far too much sorrow, the house was razed. Not a single board of it remains. The foundation was filled in and the driveway ripped up. Gone are the basketball hoop and the trampoline. Filled in with topsoil, graded and reseeded, the half-acre or so is now covered with a lush, green lawn, into which is cut a large flower garden in the shape of a heart. Neighbors and townspeople planted the garden, and in spring it bursts in yellows, reds and pinks. But no matter how it is adorned, how much love and compassion is showered upon it, the plot of land lies like a cold and empty cemetery. Life goes on in Cheshire, but it does so with the sad memory of a misty and senseless morning when the tears first began to fall.

PART I

PART I

CHAPTER ONE

3 A.M. Loose gravel on the street crunched beneath the heavy-set Hayes's feet. He could make noise in a blizzard, Joshua thought, but now Joshua wore a small smile as he shook his head and, palms facing down, motioned to his older partner to walk *softly*. Joshua was either getting used to Steven Hayes or still feeling a little bit of a buzz from the beer and Southern Comfort he'd had at the sports bar or, more likely, charged by the thrill of the crime he was about to commit. Leading the way, Joshua, younger looking than his 26 years (even considering four-and-a-half of them had been spent in jail), his frame slim with muscles like rope knots, moved silently up the driveway, into the backyard and past the sunroom. It was then that he first saw Dr. Petit, asleep on the couch in the enclosed porch. Joshua stood there motionless at the edge of complete darkness in the yard. A soft light was coming from inside the room. Hayes stood behind Joshua, anxiously shifting his weight from one foot to the other. "What are we waiting for?" Hayes said as softly as he could, but his words were nearly frantic. Joshua didn't so much as twitch. It was as if he was listening to something that only he could hear. Finally, after what must have seemed like forever to his partner, Joshua pulled a knit ski hat, with slits cut out for eyeholes, over his head. Then he turned to Hayes. "I'll let you in," he whispered.

* * *

Cheshire, Connecticut is a most unlikely setting for any murder, let alone those of a mother and her two daughters. As you turn off Interstate 84, Cheshire Road winds through a canopy of pine, elm and maple, old New England trees, descending into the fertile Naugatuck River Valley. Along this route, houses, mostly ranches and Victorians, are modest. Some show renovations made during one of the several waves of affluence that changed this town. A few still have barns in the backyards, a clue to Cheshire's farming roots. Halfway between the highway and the town center, such as it is, you'll come across a farm stand. Cheshire owns the Thornton Wilderesque title of "the Bedding Plant Capital of Connecticut." And there are still a half dozen or so working farms in and around Cheshire.

Though the soil beneath this town suits its farming heritage (and covers the remnants of barite that many years ago brought a migration of Welsh miners) the identity of Cheshire today is discovered not in the many greenhouses or the rows of corn in August, but in the cul-de-sacs and subdivisions that carve the wooded land. Cheshire is now a town of certain means, a bedroom community.

Today, the population of Cheshire is about 28,000 and the average family income is around $90,000. The city of New Haven is only 14 miles to the south, and many of Cheshire's residents work for Yale University, or in the health care industry, a major employer there. Hartford, Connecticut, is 20 miles north of Cheshire. The state capital, Hartford is to big insurance what Detroit is, or once was, to the automotive industry. The bucolic town of Cheshire is home for many insurance executives.

In 2007, the average cost of a house in Cheshire was

$330,000 and there are plenty of homes that cost much more. Most of these structures sit on manicured lawns and are fronted by sculpted bushes. In back there are redwood decks, flagstone patios and some built-in swimming pools. In the summer, the smell of charcoal and grilling steak floats from one backyard to another. At night, children leave their bikes on the front lawns with not a single worry that they will be gone in the morning. Cheshire's violent crime rate is in the lowest 1 percent of the state, and the town is near the bottom in every other major crime statistic. There are four sex offenders registered as living in Cheshire—four too many most would say, but a ratio that is far below the state's average. Though you might see a Slomin's Shield, an ADT sign, or the symbol of some other home security company, chances are, more doors in Cheshire are left unlocked than alarmed. At least that's the way it was before that late July night when two parolees broke into the home at 300 Sorghum Mill Drive. Before then, Cheshire was a trusting town.

It is also a family town. At last count, there are sixteen Little League teams in Cheshire, and far more managers and umpires in the bleachers than on the fields. Parents here take their kids' baseball seriously, and their zeal and acrimony has been the fodder for at least one *New York Times* story. The townspeople's fervency for sports is by no means limited to the 11- and 12-year-olds. The high school boys' football team has a rich history and, for many years, was among the best in the state. In 1993, the National Sports Service ranked the Cheshire Rams number one in all of New England. Though the football team has achieved much, they take a back seat to the ladies. The Cheshire girls' swimming team holds the national record for the most consecutive dual meet victories. Cheshire's wrestlers and basketball and baseball players have all collected shelves filled with trophies. And some of the local boys made good on the big sports stage. Veteran Houston Astros catcher Brad Ausmus once wore the red pinstripes of the Cheshire Rams. One of Ausmus's classmates was Brian Leech, the one-time star hockey player for the New York Rangers. When the Rangers were champions of hockey in 1994, Leech arranged for the Stanley Cup to be brought to the Cheshire Youth Center.

Yes, Cheshire is a sports town. Maybe the only thing more important here is its faith.

According to the Yellow Pages, there are nineteen places of worship in Cheshire that, along with two synagogues, span the Christian spectrum from St. Bridget's Roman Catholic to the multi-denominational First Congregational, whose spire is the official symbol of the town.

Two of the Cheshire churches especially seem to have little in common. One was the small and fervent Christ Community Church with its congregation of modest means; the other, United Methodist, with a religiously liberal and moneyed flock. And yet for our story, these two houses of worship are forever linked in the most unfortunate way. For it was the United Methodist of which the Petit family were enthusiastic members, where Jennifer Hawke-Petit taught Sunday school, where Michaela Petit, 11, sang in the church's musical programs and had just played her first flute solo, where Hayley Petit, 17, hammered nails and wielded an electric drill with the church's summer teen brigade doing home improvements for the disabled, where the whole family acted out roles each Christmas in the "Living Nativity." Mrs. Jennifer Hawke-Petit played Mary, her husband, Dr. William Petit, played a king.

And, across town, in the Baptist church, is where a young boy with a Russian last name would first learn to praise Jesus, but would turn his back on the church and ultimately bring to Cheshire its most soulless morning.

CHAPTER TWO

Joshua Komisarjevsky (pronounced Ko-mi-sor-JEFF-ski) sat in the red Chevy Venture parked in the Stop & Shop parking lot and smoked Camels. Born and raised in Cheshire, Joshua had the anonymity of a native. There was no reason for anyone to think that the nice-looking fellow with the auburn hair and the easy smile sitting behind the wheel of the red van was anything but a local guy working for a living. And he was. He worked for a roofing company out of East Hartford, and did some of his own contracting work on the side. But Joshua was not your average Cheshire workingman. He had quite a long criminal history in and around Cheshire. Those exploits, combined with his unusual last name, earned him a reputation with Cheshire police.

Just a few days prior, the monitoring bracelet attached to his ankle had been removed. The bracelet was part of his parole agreement. He had served 4-and-a-half years of a 9-year sentence for multiple home burglary charges. Though the bracelet had been removed, he was still on parole and would be until August of 2013. That is, unless he violated any of the provisions. In his newfound freedom, Joshua had already violated a number of them. And now he was about to obliterate any validity of the parole agreement.

The contractor was late. Joshua was waiting to get paid

for some work he'd done. Just one more aggravation that came with a job that he was sorry he'd taken in the first place. Joshua had worked all weekend on it, a renovation. He was supposed to have a crew of guys helping him, but they'd never shown. Each time he called the foreman to complain he was told, "They're on their way." Yeah, right. When penguins really dance, he thought.

But what bothered Joshua the most about the job was that it had taken away the time he could have spent with Jayda, his 5-year-old daughter. He knew she was in good hands, his mom's, the built-in babysitter. But still. He had just gotten custody of Jayda, and he cherished their time together: taking Jayda to work where she made an arbor for Nana (her grandmother), or in the evening when they made and ate s'mores, or at bedtime when he would read her a Bible story, just as his mother had done for him.

Instead of all that, he was framing a garage until it was too dark to see. And if the job wasn't bad enough, there was Hayes. Fucking Hayes. Bothering Joshua about the jam Hayes had, once again, found himself in. Joshua had met Hayes in a halfway house, and later they were roommates in a community release treatment center in Hartford. In those environments, Hayes was easy to like. Always with the jokes, and, as nearly a lifer behind bars, he knew the code. In a way that only ex-cons can, Joshua trusted Hayes with his back.

When Hayes was released, Joshua had put him to work on some side jobs he'd picked up. "Hey, you can teach a monkey to swing a hammer," Joshua would later say.

Anyhow, Hayes liked to work—when he was clean. When he was using, Hayes only liked to do one thing. And every time he smoked that one thing, and then found a hooker to smoke it with, it was only a matter of time before he was back in jail. How many times? Twenty-two, twenty-three convictions? Jesus!

But since his last release, Hayes was clean. At least Joshua thought he was. Dutifully, Hayes had attended the Cocaine Anonymous meeting Joshua chaired on Tuesday night in Cheshire. But now Hayes had a story. His mother was threatening to throw him out of the house, a violation of his parole agreement. Though Joshua would later say he didn't ask Hayes why his mother wanted him out, he had to know. Just a week or so before, Hayes had told him that he'd saved a couple of grand. Hayes's plan was to get a new truck. But the money had gone up in smoke. And Joshua had to have known it was crack smoke.

All that aside, when Hayes asked his halfway house roomie "to do some work," Joshua didn't hesitate. Hayes needed the money to get a place with a lease so he could show his parole officer. Without a place with a lease, it was, for sure, back to the joint. Joshua was not nearly as desperate, but still he promised to help Hayes out.

He would later say that his primary motive was to get his buddy out of a jam. But, come on, what criminal is altruistic? The very nature of crime is selfish. Sure you might pick up a running buddy to bolster your confidence, to pull jobs you'd never dare to do alone. But you're not going to put your ass on the line to bail someone else out. No, it wasn't about Hayes.

Anyhow, burglarizing houses had always meant more to Joshua than just easy money. His motives were as complex as his emotional balance, one that he would later admit drew several clinical diagnoses. Partly Joshua said yes to Hayes because he simply liked to break into houses. He would later say he was drawn by "the thrill of the crime." But Hayes also knew the buttons to push. Joshua's biggest button had "MANHOOD" stamped on it. Joshua wasn't about to let anyone question his courage. He would show this joker just how good a criminal he was.

CHAPTER THREE

At some point—it's hard to tell exactly where—Cheshire Road becomes Main Street and runs right into Maplecroft Plaza, eight acres of macadam on which sit a prefab shopping center with a Marshalls, Stop & Shop, Subway sandwiches and a branch of the Bank of America.

The shopping center stands out from the quaintness of Cheshire like a plastic lawn chair at an antique show. On any given day, in nice weather or foul, the parking lot is filled with a combination of soccer moms' SUVs and the panel and pickup trucks of Cheshire's service providers: landscapers, tree surgeons, plumbers, contractors, etc. In Cheshire, such services are always busy. One of these was the roofing company from East Hartford that employed Joshua.

As you pass Maplecroft Plaza, and the First Congregational Church, just where Main Street becomes Highland Avenue (Route 10), a gated driveway leads to a gathering of brick buildings that are nestled on a rolling lawn and among poplar trees. Cheshire Academy is Connecticut's oldest boarding school. With Episcopal roots, it counts among its alumni Abraham Lincoln's Secretary of the Navy, the author Robert Ludlum, and its most famous alum (if you don't count James Van Der Beek of *Dawson's Creek* fame), banker J. P. Morgan. Today, the school tries hard to shed its WASPy wings and prides itself on its diversity. Students from all parts of the world, as many as twenty-five countries, receive their primary and secondary education at Cheshire Academy. The school also prides itself on a faculty and staff that are not only of a high caliber, but one that places an enormous emphasis on caring for the student. Nowhere at the school is this more in evidence than in the health center, whose co-director was Jennifer Hawke-Petit.

By all accounts, Nurse Hawke-Petit brought motherly comfort to the children of Cheshire Academy—her office tended as much to homesickness as to any other malady. Robert Nuell, a student at Cheshire, knew this first-hand. In 2004, while he was an eleventh grader in the school, his grandfather passed away. A long way from family in Florida, Robert looked to the health center for comfort. "Mrs. Petit had such caring eyes," he said. "She was almost like a parent." For weeks after his grandfather died, Robert would stop in on free periods to see Mrs. Petit, sometimes spending hours with her. " 'You're going to be OK,' she kept telling me," Robert said. "I believed her."

But if the health center of Cheshire Academy represents nurturing safety, a building a mile or so north on Highland Avenue embodies the exact opposite. Without it, however, no tour of Cheshire is complete.

With its columns, brick facade and stone stairs, and the expansive slope of manicured lawn that fronts it, Cheshire Correctional Institution could easily be mistaken for a private hospital or a New England college. Don't be fooled. The structure is one of Connecticut's largest maximum-security prisons, with a history as gloomy as hell.

Built in 1910 as a reformatory when Cheshire was still a farm town of 2,000, the prison was once used by Cheshire's parents as a way of keeping their children in line. "When our kids wouldn't eat their spinach, we told them we were going to send them to the reform school," one long-time resident told a reporter.

At one time, the auditorium in the jail was used for the local high school's graduation ceremony. The audience was comprised of the graduates' families, and inmates who looked on from the back rows. No doubt, the conclusion of the event had an air of relief for the parents and graduates alike.

A retired Cheshire cop named Bill Glass who grew up in the town remembered attending Chapman Elementary School, up Highland Avenue from the prison. Often inmates would be working the prison's lawn under the wary stares of the guards. When the Chapman students would walk past, the cons were required to look down at their shovels or work shoes, and God help the inmate who made eye contact with any of the children.

But as scary as the jail was to Cheshire's children, it was nearly unbearable to the inmates within. As far back as 1932, the prison was found to be "substandard." One warden described the jail, with its long hallways and narrow cells, as a "Jimmy Cagney–type prison." Once part of the famous Sing Sing prison in Ossining, New York, the cellblock, delivered by barge, consisted of 200 eight-foot-square cells stacked four high, and was at least twice used by Hollywood as backdrop in films. The most recent, just a few months after the Cheshire murders, was a scene filmed there by Robert De Niro.

Once, inmates tended fields of potato and corn, and attended to Holsteins on prison grounds. In the old days, convicts drove plow horses. By the 1920s, the prison had a woodshop that was said to produce "cabinet work" quality— the most popular item was a cedar chest that was "purchased to hold the trousseaux linens of many a Cheshire bride," according to one newspaper article of the day. The Cheshire jail also produced license plates, 125,000 a year at peak production. By the 1980s, Cheshire Correctional had instituted vocational programs that included auto body repair, auto mechanics and food service.

Throughout the 1990s, gang violence dominated the news from within the prison walls. In the early '90s, several dangerous inmates escaped, prompting a passionate community reaction. As a result, a system of "escape notification pagers" was issued to three hundred or so families in homes surrounding the prison. But in recent conversations with Cheshire residents, the jail is hardly ever mentioned. Though it still looms like an evil castle, the most newsprint the prison now gets is the burden it puts on Cheshire's sewage system. And, for the most part, few of the thousands of cons who have served their debts to society inside the Cheshire prison have left any sort of mark on the surrounding town. That is, except for two: Steven Hayes and Joshua Komisarjevsky, both of whom spent time behind those prison walls.

CHAPTER FOUR

Joshua lit another Camel. Now there were three butts on the ground outside the van's window. A three-cigarette wait for this asswipe. Joshua smoked at least two packs of Camel non-filters a day, but would chastise anyone who dared to light up anywhere near Jayda.

In fact, Joshua was a bundle of contradictions. He drank coffee by the pot, but by his own estimation was "addicted to Mountain Dew." He was a big Guns N' Roses fan, but he also avidly listened to classical music stations, and loved Southern rock: "Can't go wrong with a little Skynyrd's 'Sweet Home Alabama'" he liked to say. Among his favorite movies he listed the saccharine *Christmas in Connecticut* as well as the gore fests *Hostel* and *Hostel Part II*. Though he was clueless on the dance floor, he adored Fred Astaire and Ginger Rogers movies. He liked to attend raves and drop acid, but he knew all about Mickey Rooney's career.

Finally a car pulled up next to Joshua's van. But even before the foreman handed him the cash, Joshua knew it was light. He could tell even before he squeezed the envelope. It was the expression worn by the foreman that gave it away. He'd seen the same look many times from customers in his marijuana-trafficking days, boys with stories, he'd say. He was right about the foreman, of course. The look never lied. *What the fuck?* Joshua said to him. In return, he got a shrug.

That's all I got, was the foreman's answer. *Maybe I can squeeze out some more, but you'll have to give me some time*.

Yeah right, Joshua thought. He'd heard those same words before too from the marijuana-moving days.

After the foreman left, Joshua just sat there and smoked another Camel. Before he went to jail in 2002, he'd smoked Marlboro Reds. He lost five years of his life by sentence and five more off his life expectancy due to the jailhouse habit. No filters. *Stop smoking*, should be the first thing they tell you after the door locks behind you, he thought.

With the envelope stuffed in the front pocket of his jeans, he was just about to back out when he caught his reflection in the rearview mirror. Joshua had eyes that belied his hardened expression. There was a nice, Christian boy's softness in Joshua's brown irises. Worked like magic with the young ladies. With the real young ladies. Worked with Caroline, his latest girlfriend, Jennifer, the mother of his child, et al. Joshua seemed to get stuck on the number 16. OK, he frequented a few hookers, went to topless bars–Gotta love those strippers, he would say. But when he had to wrap a relationship around the sex, it was only sweet 16 for Joshua. He'd dated a 16-year-old when he was 16. He'd dated and impregnated a 16-year-old when he was 22. That was Jennifer. And now, at 26, there was Caroline, again a 16-year-old. Just the thought of Caroline pulsated through Joshua like the bass guitar of a rock band.

It was at a Christian boys' summer camp on Kezar Lake in Lovell, Maine, that Joshua, then only 16 himself, sent there because of behavioral problems, first met Caroline. Seven or eight years old at the time, Caroline was the younger sister of Claire, the girl Joshua was then dating, and the daughter of a visiting pastor.

Fast-forwarding to 2002, Joshua went to jail for burglarizing houses in Bristol and Meriden, Connecticut—nineteen of them by law enforcement's count. But they only know the tip of the iceberg, he'd say. It was then that Caroline reappeared in Joshua's life. She's not sure whether she'd written to Joshua first, or if he'd written to her, and later, to confuse things even further, she would tell a reporter that the first contact they'd had was on the phone.

But regardless of how it started, a correspondence would flourish throughout Joshua's incarceration. At some point, the letters became intimate. In one way, it was a perfectly safe forum for Caroline to explore the feelings that most girls have in their middle teens. She could be as naughty as she wanted without having to worry about actually having to face her fantasies in the flesh. For Joshua, incarcerated at 22, the letters offered a sexual escape of his confines, through the writings of an eager and precocious pen pal.

Soon, Caroline was the sole object of Joshua's intentions. The letters evolved into a two-way diary. Each would mail the other their entries, which were then copied into their respective books. As Joshua's years in jail went by, the emotional and sexual tension transmitted by pen and prose accumulated. It was foreplay of the most literary kind. Caroline, the daughter of a Christian minister, a Goth girl who caved to her sexual desire. There was at least one conjugal visit, according to Caroline, after she had "turned legal," she says—16 years old in Connecticut.

When Joshua was placed in a halfway house on June 6, 2006, his first step in the parole process, the romance with Caroline exploded in a most physical way. They couldn't wait. With a halfway house furlough, Joshua would take a bus every Thursday to the Buckland Hills mall in Manchester to meet up with Caroline. There the lovers would rush into a single-occupancy bathroom, lock the door and pull each other's clothing off.

Joshua was a boyish-looking, 26-year-old ex-con. Though slender, his chest and arms were cut like rope from carrying tarpaper and bundles of shingles, his skin was brown, his auburn hair highlighted from the summer sun and his muscled back adorned with two ravens, tattoos in homage to his favorite poem by Poe.

Prompted by Joshua, Caroline also got a tattoo, of a devil. She let Joshua take dirty pictures of her on a camera phone. Caroline would shrug off their importance. Since it was her phone, she reasoned, she had control over who saw the photos. "She's anything but the innocent pastor's daughter," Joshua would later write in a letter. "Her father would have flipped his lid if he ever caught us."

Maybe Caroline's father did know, Joshua thought. Maybe that's why he dragged the whole family out to Arkansas, some town in the northwest part of the state that's famous for having the first Wal-Mart. Arkansas! And what did that leave Joshua? Cyber-sex? Downloaded cell phone pictures and dirty talk on the phone? Not like the real thing. Not by a long shot, Joshua said. Arkansas. Damn. If this weekend got any worse, Joshua didn't know what he was going to do.

CHAPTER FIVE

In comparison to some of the old money homes and the newer McMansions, the Petit house was rather modest. Worth nearly $400,000, it fell right in the middle of what houses cost in Cheshire. By any measure, though, it was a nice home, a family home. A light green, modern Colonial with a brick fireplace, it sat on a corner patch of lawn that featured, out front, a small flower garden with a rock border.

The master of the house, Dr. William Petit, Jr., liked to tend the flowers. Before the unimaginable happened, Dr. Petit, 50, had reached his middle age gracefully. There is a picture of him that was circulated widely in the press. In it, he's full-faced, perhaps carrying a couple more pounds in the middle than he would have liked. But the doctor's silver-streaked hair is full and wavy. His glasses with round frames sit on a straight nose, above a smile that once came easily, as if he had just listened to the latest joke circling the clubhouse.

Until that horrible July morning, Dr. Petit's life had seemed as though it took place under a lucky star. His home-town is Plainville, Connecticut, where his father, William Petit, Sr., was once the president of the Rotary club and ran a general store. A high school basketball star, William Petit, Jr., was one of the smartest in his class. He went on to Dartmouth College, from which he graduated cum laude. He studied medicine at the University of Pittsburgh.

It was in university when he really got lucky. Jennifer Hawke was a nurse at Children's Hospital in Pittsburgh, and he was, by his own account, "a know-it-all" third-year medical student.

Dr. Petit remembers the exact circumstances of that first encounter. It was in a corner hospital room where a child named Becky lay in bed suffering from what the doctor called "post strep and kidney problems." The young, pretty nurse began to take the child's blood pressure. The young handsome med student who had, by his own estimation, "about three minutes of experience at that point," began to interject. It became clear pretty quickly, Dr. Petit said, that his future wife knew more about pediatrics and caring for children than he did. In a firm, but sweet manner, the nurse put the resident in his place—and the romance began.

Their relationship grew quickly, as relationships tend to do with people in flowering careers—especially careers in medicine. And it was in this shared passion for healing that each knew they had found the one with whom they wanted to share the rest of their lives.

Dr. Petit remembered a young patient in the Pittsburgh hospital who had leukemia and who was being cared for by both of them. The three—doctor, nurse and patient—formed the closest of bonds. After eight weeks, numerous emotional highs and lows and a successful transplant, the boy was released from the hospital with a prognosis of a long life ahead. But he wouldn't forget the young nurse and doctor, and how much they had helped him. Twenty-five years later there was a knock on the front door of the home on Sorghum Mill Drive. The boy, now a married man, had come to visit the Petits to tell them how thankful to them he still was.

The Petits were married as William Petit's residency at the hospital came to a close. He was given only six days off for a quick honeymoon. The newlyweds spent it in Meadville, Pennsylvania, where Jennifer's father, the Reverend Richard Hawke, was the pastor of the Old Stone Church. Of French-Canadian descent, Dr. Petit is Catholic, but attended services with his family at United Methodist where "he was a member in everything but name only," said the Reverend George C. Engelhardt, who was Cheshire United Methodist's pastor for twenty-nine years.

By the mid-1980s, things continued to develop quickly in the Petits' life. When Dr. Petit received a fellowship at Yale, the couple moved to Branford, Connecticut, and Jennifer applied for a job as a medicine nurse at the famous university in New Haven. Although the opening wasn't in a field Jennifer was particularly thrilled with, she "flew through the ranks," Dr. Petit remembered, and soon was the head nurse on the pediatric adolescent floor.

Then, in 1989, Jennifer became pregnant with Hayley and the couple went house-hunting in Cheshire. They found one on Sorghum Mill Drive that was perfect.

Although it's not known exactly when the basketball backboard and hoop was placed at the head of the driveway, the reason is pretty clear. Dr. Petit had played three years of college basketball while at Dartmouth, but the hoop was undoubtedly the property of his oldest daughter. Hayley's love for the game began early in her life. A fanatic of the University of Connecticut's basketball team, Dr. Petit started taking Hayley to games when she was only 18 months old. By the time she was 10, she knew the difference between zone and man-to-man defenses. Out on the driveway, father and daughter would practice. Although dad began as the teacher, by junior year in high school, as Hayley grew in height and talent, daughter held her own, and could, now and then, take her father to the hoop. Undoubtedly, Dr. Petit got great joy out of losing those one-on-one contests. Theirs was a special relationship formed in hours spent in a shared love of basketball, together gardening in the yard, and even on the golf course, where Hayley would shoot the occasional round with her dad.

The net wasn't the only sports apparatus that held a place in the driveway, although it's doubtful Dr. Petit put the trampoline to use as often as he did the basketball hoop. No, the enclosed trampoline was the domain of his younger daughter, Michaela. Neighbors often saw the 11-year-old bouncing up and down, her ponytail flapping down and up, in the opposite direction.

Though arguably, Michaela, because of age and the time they spent together, was closer to her mother, evidence of her relationship with her father is uncovered by his nickname for her. Michaela's middle name was Rose, and her father, adding the middle syllable of "Michaela" as an initial, called her K. K. Rosebud.

"K.K. would play basketball with me, but was sort of bored watching it," Dr. Petit would later say. "And I told her this was going to be the big year, because Hayes [short for Hayley] was going to college," a journey his daughter wouldn't make. "And I said, 'Time is up, you're going to have to come to the UConn games with me, you know? You're going to have to learn how to do your homework in the car like Hayes did.'"

Still, Michaela wouldn't have been a Petit if she didn't have some love of sport. Earlier in that summer of 2007, she'd completed the "Athletic Experience" at Miss Porter's

School in Farmington, Connecticut, playing soccer, basketball and lacrosse. And it is certainly within the realm of possibility that Michaela would have happily taken Hayley's place at UConn games with her dad—if only she'd had that opportunity.

Dr. Petit had plenty to keep him busy, and plenty for which to be grateful. He was the medical director of a diabetes center, as well as the director of the section of endocrinology, metabolism and diabetes at The Hospital of Central Connecticut. Also something of a small-town doctor, Dr. Petit had a thriving private practice in his nearby hometown of Plainville.

There was seemingly only one flaw in the otherwise pretty Petit family photograph. Jennifer had been diagnosed some years earlier with multiple sclerosis. Though the illness had done little to slow her down, MS is known to be progressive, and is still without a cure.

For the Petits, Jennifer's disease actually worked to bring a close family even closer. Just after her mother was diagnosed with MS, Hayley organized and captained a fundraising walk team that she called "Hayley's Hope." In seven years, from age 10 to 17, Hayley's Hope raised over $55,000. When Hayley graduated from high school, she handed over the reins of the team to Michaela, who promptly changed the name to "Michaela's Miracle."

Along with raising money, the sisters also assisted their mother in more subtle ways, sometimes just by holding Jennifer's hand when she would have a reaction to her medication. "Now that I'm older," Hayley said in a speech at an MS fund-raiser, "I realize there are many little things I can do to help my mom."

So close were mother and daughters that Dr. Petit would

have to remind his wife that she was not their sister. "She
was their confidante," he would later say. Jennifer may have
relied on her daughters for support, but when life would turn
in the most horrible way, she would also prove to be fearless
in trying to protect them.

CHAPTER SIX

Joshua turned the key in the van and it rumbled to life. Piece of crap. In his salad days, when he was moving pounds of pot from the Canadian border south all the way to Virginia, when he got all his friends high and spent money like a jackpot winner at Foxwoods, he had a 1998 red-and-silver Chevy Silverado. Now *that* was a truck. He liked to take it up to the White Mountains and rip up an old logging road. And here he was sitting in a bucket of bolts. Even Caroline giggled at the sight of it. He jabbed the PLAY button on the CD player. One of his favorite songs, the Guns N' Roses ballad "November Rain" filled the cab.

Now he was really feeling sorry for himself. It was a mindset in Joshua that was always the first step down on a staircase that would end in a basement of serious depression.

Joshua had a long history of depression. When he was 14 he was sent to Elmcrest psychiatric hospital in Portland, Connecticut, after committing several crimes including burglary and arson. While he was hiding from the cops in the woods of his grandfather's estate, he'd cut the word "HATE" into his forearm with a hunting knife. He had also left a suicide note. According to court documents, Joshua's parents had only grudgingly gone along with the directive to send their son for psychiatric help. Fervent Christians, Ben and Jude Komisarjevsky thought prayer was the answer to Joshua's problems.

A lawyer who represented Joshua told a court that the Komisarjevksys had taken their son out of the hospital against better judgment and placed him in a "faith program." The attorney, William Gerace, also said that Joshua's parents thought the anti-depressants the hospital had prescribed were "a crutch," and refused to let their son take them. Later, at the same hearing, Jude Komisarjevsky refuted Gerace. She said that the hospital had released Joshua, and that she and her husband were afraid that their son would overdose on the medication. Joshua had a history of suicide attempts, documented in court records.

But in front of the Stop & Shop, Joshua had something else on his mind besides the foreman, Axl Rose or even Caroline. A Chrysler Pacifica minivan occupied by three females parked right next to him.[1]

The door to the van opened. It was a mother and daughter, he could tell, though the mother was blonde and youthful. The daughter was almost as tall as her mother, her hair pulled back in a ponytail. Joshua watched as they walked together towards the store. The girl was pretty, her skin brown from the summer sun. Joshua would later say that it was the Petits' minivan that caught his attention, signaling to him that here was a family with money. But on any given afternoon, the Stop & Shop parking lot in Cheshire is filled with Lexus

---

[1] Early news stories would report that only Jennifer and Michaela were in the minivan, but Joshua contends that Hayley was in the automobile too, and that she'd stayed in the car while her mother and sister went shopping.

and BMW SUV's. As the mother and daughter disappeared into the store, Joshua turned off the Venture, raised his combat boot–clad foot and rested it against the dashboard, leaned back in his seat and waited.

CHAPTER SEVEN

That summer had been a transitional one for both of the Petit girls. Hayley had just concluded her four years at Miss Porter's School. Sometimes students just call it "Farmington" for the Connecticut town in which it is located, probably because "Miss Porter's" sounds as prudish as it does antiquated. The school is somewhat unfairly categorized—mentioned in several films, Broadway shows and works of fiction—as a debutante academy. Some of its famous alumni, Jacqueline Bouvier and Gloria Vanderbilt, for two, did little to dispel that reputation.

But there is nothing easy about attending Miss Porter's. According to its mission statement, the school challenges its students to become informed, bold, resourceful, and ethical global citizens. "We expect our graduates to shape a changing world," pronounces the school's website. In Hayley's senior year, the mean SAT score for Miss Porter's students was Math 617/Verbal 617/Writing 620, no easy accomplishment by any measure. The school's graduates attend the best colleges in the country. Although academics is a school priority, Miss Porter's is also known for its sports. Just like her dad, Hayley excelled in both arenas.

Although never a high scorer on Miss Porter's basketball team, a testament to her unselfishness, Hayley Petit was consistently a top rebounder and shot blocker. One of her idols was Swin Cash, a WNBA star who had led the UConn Huskies to two national titles on the strength of her rebounding (and prolific scoring, sixth all-time at UConn). Hayley had a poster of Cash on her bedroom wall.

In her senior year Hayley broke her left hand, and missed fifteen games—almost the entire season. When she returned, she did so in a flourish, blocking nine or ten shots and helping lead the team to a victory. "She led by example," her father would later say.

That senior year, Hayley was the captain of the basketball team as well as captain of the crew team. She rowed in the first boat in both her junior and senior years. There's a move in crewing called "the power ten." It's something of an all-out maneuver used only when a boat falls behind. According to Dr. Petit, in Hayley's senior year the freshman team renamed the move to "the Hayley ten," in her honor. If crewing and basketball weren't enough, Hayley also ran cross-country.

Even in her stocking feet, Hayley was what would, a couple of generations back, be called "statuesque." A bit uncomfortable with her height, Hayley was self-conscious around boys. For the junior prom, one friend, who attended a different high school, tried to set Hayley up with a towering basketball player, but for some reason the pairing didn't click. Now and then her dad would tease her about some boy she seemed interested in, and Hayley would turn crimson in embarrassment.

And it wasn't as if she couldn't have her pick. "She woke up looking great," said Megan Alexander, Hayley's life-long friend. According to Megan, Hayley wasn't big on make-up, and fashion didn't exactly make her go giddy. Not that she dressed badly, it was just that she was perfectly happy in jeans and flip-flops, so much so, her mother would have to remind her to put on a dress now and then.

When friends would get the idea to go to the mall and encourage her to go along, Hayley would be like, "Whatever," and not the Valley Girl version of *Whatever* either. Her reaction was more of a shrug. She might end up going to the mall, but more for the company than anything else.

Bookish and shy as a young student, Hayley received only one complaint from her teachers at Miss Porter's, and that was that they wished she would speak up more.

She might have been reserved, but her intelligence was anything but. Megan Alexander remembers an assignment in St. Margaret's, a middle school they both attended, to memorize fifty different muscles in the body. "Hayley got a hundred," said Megan with amazement.

On the last Petit family vacation, Hayley brought seven books to read, including one on oil and energy. "I don't know how many seventeen-year-olds take that on vacation," Dr. Petit would say. On that trip to Cape Cod, Dr. Petit asked Hayley to read the first three or so chapters to him out loud so he could stay awake behind the wheel. The next morning at the vacation house, Dr. Petit asked his daughter how she was progressing with the book. "I'm done," she said.

Dr. Petit admits readily that Hayley was smarter than him. She also loved to write, and became the co-editor of *Chautauqua*, the school's newspaper.

But as her high school years folded quickly one into the other, Hayley would find her voice and footing. "Hayley was a leader publicly and privately," said Burch Ford, Hayley's adviser at Miss Porter's, to a reporter. "Her profile was very high, and her presence was profoundly felt, but this was all particularly true without her ever calling attention to herself." A spokeswoman for the National Multiple Sclerosis Society told a local reporter that the Petit sisters were the top family fund-raising team in Connecticut. There is video on the Internet of a speech Hayley gave to the Rotary club, of which her grandfather was a member for forty years. She stood straight and spoke with confidence. She had an easy and fetching smile. Her hair was long and full. She looked like her dad. And even as his daughter grew into a beautiful young woman, Dr. Petit called her "Daddy's little girl."

That Hayley wanted to follow her father into medicine was not surprising at all. On her 4th birthday, Hayley received a doctor's bag complete with a child's stethoscope and other instruments. Years later, in a college application essay, she remembered the occasion. She titled the essay simply "My Dad," and in it she described trailing behind her father's white coattails as he made his rounds through the hospital on Saturdays. She was fascinated by his confidence, how he always made his patients laugh, and how he possessed a "God-like" power to heal them. "His presence made the hospital seem a fortress and anyone within its walls safe," she wrote.

Hayley's years at Miss Porter's went by in an instant—at least that's the way it seemed to her parents. On a Sunday in the middle of June 2007, the Petits held a graduation party for Hayley in the backyard. About fifty friends, school chums and family attended. But the guest of honor almost didn't make it.

In junior year, right after a track meet in which she competed, Hayley suffered a collapsed lung. Doctors said that it was just a case of her growing too fast. The lung was inflated and though the event was given sufficient attention, no one, including her doctor father, was all that concerned. But when Hayley sustained another collapsed lung just before graduation, this one seemingly random, she found herself in New Briton General, the hospital out of which Dr. Petit worked, being prepared for an operation.

The defect was genetic, they were told. And though the prospect of the operation being a complete success was high, the procedure needed to be done right away.

Hayley's biggest concern was whether she'd be able to go to her own party. Many of her classmates lived far afield—across the country and even around the world. It might be her last chance to see them. "She worked hard to make the party," said Megan Alexander.

Hayley did make it, in spite of the fact that she still had tubes in her lungs. Though she was in extreme discomfort, she smiled a gracious smile throughout. In fact, "wearing a white sundress, she looked gorgeous," said Megan.

One of Hayley's favorite television shows was *Dr. Quinn, Medicine Woman*. Her father once gave her a boxed DVD set of the series. It was Hayley who suggested the name "Michaela" when her mom was pregnant with her baby sister, that being Dr. Quinn's first name.

In July, halfway through the magical transitional summer between high school and college, Hayley's dreams were just getting started. She had applied and received early admittance to Dartmouth, where she planned to study pre-med. She already had her sights set on crewing for the college rowing team.

And still other adventures lay ahead. Though friends remember Hayley having a few "crushes," there wasn't a steady boyfriend in her life. Part of the reason was that she went to an all-girls' school—that and the fact that she was "way too busy," says Megan Alexander. "She probably would've had plenty of opportunity in college."

Michaela, too, had big things in store the next school year. But first there was summer to be enjoyed. Along with participating in Athletic Experience at Miss Porter's, Michaela spent hers with her family at Cape Cod and going to the club to which the Petits belonged.

It had been a good vacation season. She had continued to educate her epicurean palate by watching Rachael Ray, eating vegetarian and going to the mall with her grandmother for root beer floats. By family accounts, Michaela was devoted to The Food Channel. Dr. Petit often found himself watching his beloved Huskies or some other Big East tilt on the television in his upstairs study while Michaela commandeered the remote for the downstairs TV for a replay of *Iron Chef*'s finale or some other foodie show. That is, unless Dr. Petit had had an extraordinarily hard day, and then he'd pull rank, he would later say.

An aspiring singer (at least along to the radio), she liked to entertain family and friends with her road trip vocals. "She was the kind of kid that would hear a song once in the car and she would know it and sing it on-key," her father would later say. "Her mom could sing as well. Hayley and I were kind of squawkers off-key," Dr. Petit said. Mom played the piano. Michaela played the flute.

In photos, Michaela always wears a smile that gleams with braces. Some casual images show her blonde hair in a ponytail; in dress-up photos, her hair is long and brushed to a gleaming shine.

Her father said that, as a very young girl, Michaela had been on the chubby side. He related one anecdote where she'd come home crying after a classmate had pointed to her tummy and inquired, "What's that?" But Michaela sprouted when she began to attend school, and was taller and looked older than most of her peers. Dr. Petit remarked that she could easily pass for 14, when she was only 11.

Like her older sister, Michaela was shy. Her father said that she had a penchant for looking at her feet when introduced to someone new. But then, he said, she would raise her head and smile in such a genuine way, all but the most stoic souls were drawn in.

Michaela was going into sixth grade at Chase Collegiate School, a private day school in Waterbury, Connecticut, that traces its roots back to the 1860s. She was following the educational path of her older sister (St. Margaret's had changed its name to Chase Collegiate). And like her older sister, she was in a summer of transition. New and exciting worlds lay ahead. Though boys were still a strange and icky lot, there are indications that the world of crushes and holding hands was on the horizon. There are photographs of Michaela from a friend's 10th birthday party where the girls gave each other makeovers. In one of the photos, Michaela, wearing makeup and sporting large sunglasses, looks more like a college freshman on spring break than a sixth grader. But sleepover party makeovers are really just children playing dress-up. And in most of the pictures, her smile is one common in children with braces: self-conscious but very sweet.

Though it seemed that Michaela couldn't wait to reach her teens, she was still very attached to her mother, and spent much of her time away from school at the Cheshire Academy. The academy encouraged visits by faculty and staff family members, and Michaela took full advantage. Her best friend's parents worked at the academy, and Michaela and her friend were often seen riding their bikes around the grounds or playing on the swing set. Mom Petit displayed Michaela's "picture of the week," a crayon drawing from school, on a wall at the health center. Co-workers and students alike came to expect the "newsflash" of Michaela's latest endeavors that Mrs. Petit would deliver. And often, she would invite students back to the Petit home, where they would get information about Michaela right from the source.

* * *

Undoubtedly there were moments when Dr. Petit would let
his gaze linger on his daughters, when he would marvel at
how quickly their childhoods had passed. The way Hayley's
hair fell, her lovely cheekbones, high like her mother's, the
sparkle in her eyes, her smile demure, he would look at her
and have to catch his breath. Maybe even more halting was
his youngest. Oh my Lord, only a moment ago was she in his
arms, an infant, now she was sprinting towards her teens. He
wanted to reach and hold her back, slow her down, like he
had when she'd learned to a ride a bicycle. But he knew from
the experience he gained from Hayley that there would be
no slowing down. Time dissolves before your eyes, especially when watching your children grow.

But that Sunday, July 22, Dr. Petit had no reason to dwell
on the past or fret about the quickness of the future. No, for
Dr. Petit everything was just fine right here and now. He had
played golf that afternoon with his father at the century-old
Country Club at Farmington. It was a perfect day, low 80s,
little humidity, a cool northeasterly breeze. The night before,
temperatures had dropped into the high 50s, and golfers
who'd teed up early were layered in sweaters and wind shirts.
If he got home in time, he no doubt watched a bit of the Red
Sox game—Manny Ramirez hit a three-run homer in the
first, and the Sox held on to beat Chicago.

Mom and Michaela had begun the day at church and then
moved on to the club to which the Petits belonged. They
were brown from the sun. Hayley had just come back from
Cape Cod, where she'd spent the weekend with some gal
pals from Miss Porter's. That evening, Michaela announced
that she was making dinner, one of her favorites—the simple
fare included a pasta dish with homemade sauce and a salad
with Cheshire-grown tomatoes and balsamic dressing, the

only dressing that Michaela used. She'd learned to cook the sauce from Mom, who, according to several sources, made the best in the universe. But Michaela needed some provisions. A trip to Stop & Shop was in order. The girls and Jennifer piled into the family's Pacifica.

With the girls on their way to the supermarket, the house was quiet, and in those moments, no doubt, Dr. Petit found comfort in the safety and warmth that he had created. In many respects, his was the perfect family, at least the suburban Connecticut version of that American dream. Still, in a life that was as busy as a full waiting room, Dr. Petit might have enjoyed time alone. Moments like these were few and far between, when a man could pad around his own house in athletic socks, and sneak a cookie out of the cupboard, a beer from the fridge—or just relax. More likely he was an uncomfortable bachelor and soon became anxious for his girls to come home.

CHAPTER EIGHT

Joshua struck a stick match and held it for a moment in front of him. The flame reflected in his brown eyes, which watched the front door of the supermarket. Michaela, holding a paper bag of groceries, appeared in the doorway, her mother right behind her. It was at that precise moment, Joshua remembers, that his cell phone rang. "It really was *the perfect storm*," he would later say, echoing an Associated Press newspaper headline that would follow the murders. He looked at the caller I.D., then flipped open the phone and pressed the cell to the side of his head. The familiar voice came over the receiver.

Got any ideas for tonight?

Not more than fifteen feet in front of him, the mother and daughter climbed into the Pacifica.

"Maybe," Joshua answered.

The minivan began to back out of the parking spot.

"Lemme get back to you."

Joshua turned the ignition key and slipped the gearshift into DRIVE. As the Petit family van neared the exit of the parking lot, Joshua began to follow.

Joshua had grown up on his grandfather's estate, a large tract of wooded land in the southwestern part of Cheshire. He tells a story of how he'd first learned to track animals. He was

6 years old when he climbed the stone wall that ran in front of his grandfather's house. From the top of the wall, he'd grabbed hold of the low-hanging branch of an oak. With one hand over the other, his heart beating hard, and careful not to look down, he climbed to the top of the 100-foot tree.

The second time he climbed the tree, a few days later, just after the 32 Bus had dropped him home from Norton Elementary, it was not nearly as scary. In no time, he was fearless.

The oak that he scaled was one of six that had once lined the road. The branches of the towering oaks intertwined to form one long canopy. He came to be able to leap from tree to tree, navigating his way along the branches, like a "red squirrel," he would say, from the northernmost oak to the one farthest to the south. That tree had the best view of his grandfather's estate.

It was from the vantage of the southernmost towering oak that one day Joshua happened to see a flock of wild turkey in the tall grass below. While he was watching the turkeys, lined up and marching like an army platoon, something ahead in the grass captured his attention. When he tried to locate the cause of the movement, however, the grass seemed only to ripple in the breeze. Then he saw it move again.

According to Joshua, Cali (short for Calico), his grandfather's cat, had a Napoleonic complex. "She thinks she's a mountain lion," he said. In a stalking belly crawl, Cali came from upwind and circled abreast of the birds until she was downwind. Joshua was mesmerized by Cali's movements: "Slow, stop, slow, stop, adjust for their westerly direction, slow, stop, slow, stop," he would remember.

The cat crawled within a few feet of the lead bird, then froze like a statue and waited for the turkey to come to her. Cali then sprang from the three-foot grass and onto the back of the bird, clawing and biting at the feathers. Joshua remembers that the turkey was "ten times the size" of his grandfather's cat, and easily shook the enraged animal from his back and made good a fast and frightened getaway. But Joshua had learned a lesson.

He would practice the technique on deer on his grandfather's estate. He became so proficient that he once was almost gored by an unsuspecting four-point buck that practically walked right into him. "Jumping behind a birch tree is all that saved me," Joshua wrote.

Later in life, Joshua would take to jingling his car keys when he came up from behind on someone. Several times he had scared people "half to death" as he just seemed to appear in their presence. He would also later implement Cali's technique in another fashion. In burglarizing houses in his early teens, he would cut a back screen door, and stand in the doorway listening for a half hour or more before entering the house: *Stop, slow, stop* . . . He became so confident in his stealth, he once watched television in a house that he had broken into while his victims slept in an upstairs bedroom. And that was only in his early teens. As he grew into a man, his burglarizing techniques became so brazen, so outrageous, that even seasoned police veterans would find them hard to believe.

Joshua lagged behind the Pacifica as it pulled from the Stop & Shop parking lot. He took his time as he watched the distance between him and the Petits' minivan increase. He wasn't even sure if the Pacifica had turned on Edwards Road or Laurel Terrace. It didn't matter. He knew they had to be headed towards Cornwall Avenue. Joshua pressed down on the gas pedal, and caught sight of the Pacifica, just as it turned off Cornwall onto Mountain Road. He was several car lengths back when the minivan turned onto Sorghum Mill Drive.

In the eighteen years she had lived in Cheshire, Jennifer Petit had driven this route countless times. She did it automatically, without thinking. So, of course, she gave not a second thought to the red van now right behind her. Why would she? It would have been more likely for the Petit girls to think that the Pacifica was about to be hit by lightning than for them to have the slightest inkling that they were being followed by someone who was formulating a plan to take them hostage.

As they pulled into the driveway at 300 Sorghum Mill Drive, and as the red van rolled slowly by, they couldn't have had any idea of the horror that night would hold.

CHAPTER NINE

The voice on Joshua's cell phone belonged to Steven Hayes, his new partner in crime, in a brand-new business venture that had begun the night before. Late that Saturday night, Joshua had picked up Hayes and cruised around Cheshire in the Chevy Venture looking for a house or houses to burglarize.

On the surface, Steven Hayes and Joshua Komisarjevsky had little in common. "I don't know why they clicked," said one halfway house resident to a local reporter. "Josh was quiet, timid, weird. Steve was outgoing, spontaneous, a little perverted." Standing together, they looked like a comedy team: Joshua the straight man, Hayes, 18 years older, delivering the punch lines. Where Joshua was wiry, rake-thin with a mop of auburn hair, Hayes was flabby and completely bald, known to halfway-house pals, and, later, Joshua's friends, as "Uncle Fester," after the hairless character from the *Addams Family* television show. Joshua could be sphinx-like in his silence; Hayes was a backslapper and a joker. Though he actually received a GED in the Cheshire jail, Hayes bragged that he'd earned his diploma "on the street"; Joshua, on the other hand, says he once scored 150 on a Stanford-Binet intelligence test, and, according to court records, had a photographic memory. As a criminal, Hayes was as predictable as a clock, the primary reason that he had been arrested twenty-three times; Joshua was only caught and sent to jail because of a trace on some items he'd stolen that showed up at a pawnshop—that, and a drug dealer he knew who'd given him up to the police.

But the shared experience of jail and halfway house took precedent over differences in taste, intellect or personality. This trust in one another was as strong as blood, especially out in a world they both perceived as aligned against them. They were brothers in the code of the convict.

Along with looking for suitable houses to break into, the ride through Cheshire that Saturday night was also something of a victory lap for Joshua as he pointed out to his new accomplice his past conquests.

By his own estimation, Joshua had broken into 1,300 houses during his burglary career. Joshua is prone to exaggeration— but even if that number is greatly inflated, he was still a prolific burglar. He committed many of his crimes simply for sport, just to see if he could pull them off successfully. In an interview in jail, he says that he broke into Tommy Hilfiger's Greenwich, Connecticut, house because he had read about the extensive security system the designer installed and wanted to see if it could be foiled[2].

Only once did Joshua come close to getting caught in the act: He didn't realize that a woman was awake, sitting in a darkened room he'd entered. She screamed, and he ran out of the house so fast, he missed the front step and fell flat on his face onto a flagstone walkway.

He was so brazen, he took to walking into houses right through the front door during dinnertime. "Everybody in the house would be in one room, with their minds on one

---

[2] Hilfiger's public relations office did not return calls to confirm or deny this.

thing—it was the best time," he would later say. He would
then hide in the basement for hours, until his victims were in
bed. He told police that he liked to hear the rhythmic breathing of his victims' sleep.

Some of his prey never even knew he was there, for he
would take nothing. Other times he would rearrange furniture
or pictures on the walls. "I liked fucking with them," he says.

Joshua called breaking into houses "a form of extreme
sport," like the mountain biking or snowboarding he enjoyed. He also didn't try to keep it a secret. "Everyone knew
I was burglar, all of my friends and the police too," he would
later boast.

But having people know in a general way is one thing,
and being able to point out the homes he'd broken into and
narrate the details to an appreciative audience was something else. He bragged that he had burglarized houses in all
the affluent neighborhoods in west Cheshire, along Mountain Road, near the Darcy and Norton schools and the Chapman School neighborhood.

When he was finally caught back in 2002, he told the
court he had experienced an epiphany. He confessed to the
burglaries the cops didn't know about because he felt a need
to unburden himself. A new father, it was the sight of his
little girl's face that had made him want to change, he says.
He wanted to do his time and then start anew—for his daughter's sake.

He'd held Jayda for the first time in a closed secondary
courtroom after one of his appearances. "[Her] bright sapphire eyes penetrated this broken man to his soul," he remembers.

But when he took the cops around, showing them house
after house that he'd burglarized, a tour that filled 10 pages
of a police report, he felt almost a childlike glee, a pride in

his craft. "They [the cops] were astounded," he would later recall with eyes glowing in delight. Months after the events in Cheshire, in a letter from jail, he bragged at length about his criminal expertise:

> *I've scaled the outside of buildings, repelled [sic] off roofs to windows or balconies below, kicked in doors, simply walked in, snorkled and dived up to buildings along canals, manipulated my way past doormen and receptionist, bribed and coerced but generally I simply observed . . . I've entered structures through doors, windows (any story), sky-lights, gable vents, ceilings, ventilation ducts, walls, elevator shafts, hell—if I knew a pilot I'd sky dive onto some of my objectives (It would have saved me lots of energy used climbing) . . . I've broken into judges houses, state police, local police (one was a state police K-9—he and his dog were home) the rich and affluent, the upper middle class, and middle class; drug dealers to investment bankers, lawyers to doctors; vacation homes to estates, condos to warehouses, department stores to small business—whatever, I enjoy the challenge.*

Back on the dark streets of Cheshire, Joshua turned off of Highland Avenue and onto Country Club Road, a route that connects Cheshire with Yalesville to the east. It is also a road that is lined with fairly affluent homes and quiet developments: the perfect hunting grounds. Joshua, of course, knew the area well, and not only as a native Cheshian. He had burglarized dozens, scores of houses here from the time he was 13 years old. For Joshua, robbing houses in Cheshire was like going to visit friends.

From Highland Avenue, Creamery Road climbs a small wooded hill on the top of which, on the right, is Country Club Road. Two blocks South on Country Club is a cul-de-sac. Joshua turned into the small quiet street, Glenbrook Drive, and saw what he was looking for. The house, the largest on the block, was just as inviting as it had been the night he'd broken into it twelve years earlier. He took one loop around Glenbrook Drive. In back a wooded tract fell quickly to a park and Route 10—the perfect escape path if need be. Joshua turned to Hayes and asked: You ready?

Throughout the tour, Hayes was chatty and excited. He liked Joshua, liked his company, although he thought his young partner was a little too intense with his extended vocabulary and peculiar interests—like ancient Greek architecture, for Christ's sake! But the kid was smart, there was no doubt about that, and maybe he was just smart enough to get Hayes out of the jam he was in. Shit, even if half of what the kid bragged about was true, he had a better chance betting on Joshua than trying to get out of it himself. Twenty-three times he'd come up with big ideas, and all of them had led to an arrest. Hayes was excited at the possibility of things turning out differently this time.

Joshua was chatty too, smiling at Hayes's cracks and nodding along. But then, out of nowhere, he got as quiet and hard as a stone. Joshua has moods. First his voice gets detached and then his stare drops as though he's looking at something on the tip of his nose. And it doesn't matter where he is or who he's with, when that look comes, he goes someplace far away. Caroline talked about it, the look. They'd be walking together in, like, Home Depot, holding hands, all warm and everything, and then he'd just drop her hand, get the look, and walk off like she was never there. She even had an expression for it: "When he flipped his lid," is what she called those moments.

But as Joshua parked the Venture in a condominium complex off Country Club Road, it was Hayes's turn to become uncharacteristically quiet. "He was nervous, and sweating," Joshua remembers. Joshua was quiet too, but his reticence was all about focus.

As they came up from around the back of the house, Hayes tromped through the thicket like a farm animal, and Joshua began to wonder if he had made a mistake taking him on as a partner. The trek through the woods led to the backyard. Joshua told Hayes to wait behind the tree line. He wasn't about to trust Hayes with this part of the job, at least not yet. Joshua didn't like depending on anyone else when he was making his night moves, and entering a house took all of his concentration and senses. He didn't want to be worrying about Hayes and figuring out how to get in at the same time.

But as it turned out, entering this house was a cinch. In fact, it all came back to him like a déjà vu moment. Joshua says he threw a towel over a motion detector he spotted, and then saw that the back window had been left open. He was in the house in a few seconds, and the next moment was waving Hayes in through the back door.

According to news stories, there were five people asleep upstairs: Ron Bergamo, his wife and 12-year-old son, and another couple. "We aren't the quaint town anymore," Mr. Bergamo would say to local reporters.

Joshua remembered that Hayes was even more nervous once inside the house. A couple of times he bumped into furniture or his weight made the floor creak under his footstep. Joshua pressed a finger to his lips and rolled his eyes at each sound.

They went through drawers and closets. Joshua removed a photograph of the Bergamo family. He would later say that he wanted Hayes to know what he might confront should somebody awaken. But Joshua had a preoccupation with who was asleep in the bedrooms of the houses he burglarized.

And this time it might have been more than just curiosity. That afternoon, Joshua had bought a BB pistol from a local sporting goods store and sawn off the tip of the barrel. A cat burglar for all of his career, the gun signaled a serious step in a violent direction. He also had picked up plastic zip ties.

Maybe Hayes was thinking of more than just a burglary too. At one point, he took a carving knife from one of the drawers. Joshua would later downplay the significance of the knife. "He just started to fool around with it," Joshua says. And Joshua had stolen knives out of homes before. One of them had belonged to a man and his then-pregnant wife. "I'm just glad I didn't run into him," the man told a local reporter. But, considering what would happen the following night, one has to wonder whether Hayes had in fact taken the knife for just a laugh.

In the Bergamo house, as time went by, Hayes began to gain confidence, smiling and quietly joking. But his humor disappeared at the sound of a car pulling into the driveway. Joshua says that he thought that Saturday night might have been prom night in Cheshire, and that perhaps one of the children was returning home from the dance. The newly formed burglar team made a quick exit out the back door.

The take from the Bergamo house was thin. According to reports, they took some cash, $140 in a money clip, but not nearly enough to help Hayes out with his problem.

For Joshua, the night still held opportunity. There were times he'd broken into three, four houses in a row. He liked to improvise. He led Hayes across the dark stillness of Glenbrook Drive to the home of David Hicks.

If getting into the Bergamo house was easy, Joshua entered the Hicks home was like he was part of the family. "I walked right through an open back door. Gotta love Cheshire," he would later say. Though Joshua remembers the house being furnished like a bachelor's pad, with a Foosball table and pinball machine, David Hicks lived there with his wife and three children, according to reports. "What happened to them [the Petits] could have happened to us," Mr. Hicks would tell a reporter.

In the Hicks home, Hayes and Joshua took their time. They found credit cards, cash and a cell phone. They also stole a photograph of the family.

In the following weeks, the Hickses would be haunted by the thought that Hayes and Joshua had taken the picture in order to target them. "That's one thing that is really bothering us," Mr. Hicks would say just after the crime. But Joshua would later say that he'd taken the photograph only to again show Hayes who was in the house. "It's information a burglar needs to know," Joshua says. Perhaps.

The amount of money they stole from the Hickses' home was no better than what they got from the Bergamos'. Although he had no right to, given the paltry amounts of money he'd been arrested for stealing in his criminal career as a smash-and-dash thief, Hayes started to get annoyed. In Hayes's eyes, they were taking a huge risk for chump change. An arrest would send him back to jail for a very long time.

But as far as Joshua was concerned, there was practically no risk involved. For him, this first night with Hayes as his partner wasn't a total loss at all. All things considered, Hayes hadn't done badly as a first-time burglar. There was part of Joshua that exulted in the mentor's role, and he began to see the night as sort of a training exercise. It was another way for him to show off his skills. Tomorrow's another day, Joshua would tell Hayes. And, at least for that moment, Hayes was the perfect pupil and willing to wait.

As they made their way back to the van, Joshua thought that maybe a partnership with Hayes had possibilities. Practice makes perfect, Joshua thought. As it happened, the partnership between Steven Hayes and Joshua Komisarjevsky would last only one more night, and they would only break into one more house.

CHAPTER TEN

That Sunday, after he followed the Pacifica to Sorghum Mill Drive, Joshua drove back to his parents' house, where he fed Jayda and then prepared her bath.

That day she'd worn the little toy tool belt he'd bought her. She's gonna make a wonderful contractor, he would later say. Sitting on her father's lap as he worked a backhoe, she'd scream in glee: "Daddy, daddy, let me dig the hole, wait for meee!"

She'd been conceived, according to Joshua, in a cabin near a lake in New Hampshire. Joshua would later remember the moment when he first experienced a father's love for his child. Jennifer, fully pregnant with Jayda, was asleep and curled in Joshua's arms. At the time, he was awaiting a court date in Virginia, where he'd been busted with somewhere around five pounds of marijuana. Connecticut police also wanted to talk to him about two burglaries he'd committed—two that they knew about. He had found out about the cops' interest in him when a detective called his mother's house pretending to be from Motor Vehicles. Not exactly Hercule Poirot, the detective had his true identity uncovered by Mrs. Komisarjevsky's caller I.D., which read "POLICE DEPARTMENT." Joshua knew that it was only a matter of time before the authorities caught up to him. But for that one moment, with Jennifer in his arms, he felt what fathers have felt forever. As he would later write,

> *This moment etched so deep in my heart, watching her sleep in peaceful bliss, feeling our soon to be newborn daughter brought me to tears.*

A few months later, Joshua would stand in front of a judge waiting to be sentenced. Jennifer, with infant Jayda in her arms, would sit in the courtroom behind him. The judge asked if he had anything to say. "The crimes I committed was weighing so heavily on my shoulders that when the police did approach me that day, I explained to them and sat down with them and told them why and what I did, the other crimes that I did and why I did them," Joshua said, his voice breaking. "And the only reason why I did it was because my daughter was supposed to be born within the week, and I wanted a chance to start over and to start a new leaf, I guess you could say. I only pray that I have the opportunity to be able to raise my daughter in the love and the faith that now has new meaning to my life."

For a moment, it seemed as though the judge might have compassion for Joshua and his situation, and show leniency. But if Joshua experienced even the slightest amount of hope that somehow he would sidestep a jail sentence, the judge quickly dispelled that notion when he called Joshua "a calculated, cold-blooded predator," and then went on to say, ". . . you're violating people's home at night, and that's when people are most vulnerable, when they're sleeping, and at least one of those cases involved a home where there were children." Just before the judge brought down the gavel, his final statement to Joshua was this: "I would hope that you would use the next fifteen years to better yourself so that you're not back before a court, facing sentencing on similar charges."

But throughout his time in prison, Joshua would profess his love for Jayda. At one point visiting rights were curtailed because of the use of children in smuggling drugs into the prison. In a letter written in jail to a friend, Joshua would lament his situation:

> ... *it very difficult for those of us who legitimately wish to hold and spend time with our children. My daughter knows who I am and knows the sound of my voice. She calls me daddy and tells me she loves me but I haven't seen her for awhile.*

And now, with Jayda not yet 5 years old, he was watching her splash around the tub. After he dried, powdered and dressed his daughter in pajamas, Joshua left Jayda in his mother's care and went outside for a smoke. He was unyielding in his rule that his daughter not be subjected to second-hand smoke, and anyone who knew Joshua didn't dare smoke anywhere near his daughter.

While he was outside, a car pulled up.

The day before, on Saturday afternoon, Joshua had taken Jayda to a playground just across from Cheshire High School. While he watched his daughter play in the sandbox, Joshua had caught a glance from a young woman there with two small children of her own. It took them each a moment to recognize one another. "Are you Josh?" the woman finally asked. Joshua had grown up with Sarah, who was the daughter of a waitress in town.

It was Sarah in the car that pulled up in front of the house. They talked for some time. "I had a feeling she was interested," Joshua would later say with a sly smile about Sarah's follow-up visit. Though he was intrigued, by this time, Joshua began to feel the need for more immediate excitement. His thoughts went to Caroline, and the pictures of her on his computer. He walked into the house and carried Jayda to bed, where he read her a Bible story. Then he sat on his own bed and opened his laptop.

CHAPTER ELEVEN

On Sorghum Mill Drive, Michaela's dinner, served family-style, was a hit. At some point during that evening, perhaps right after dinner, given the hysteria of the just-released volume, the girls reposed to their bedrooms where each was deeply engrossed in J. K. Rowling's latest work—though for Hayley, reading "Harry Potter" was more of a "time out" from her preferred, more substantive reading matter, a friend would later surmise. Still, as the older sister, Hayley had first dibs, and was well into *Harry Potter and the Deathly Hallows*, while Michaela was finishing the next-to-last installment, *Harry Potter and the Half-Blood Prince*, all the while looking forward to getting her turn at the grand finale in her sister's hands.

After the requisite phone calls and emails, the last chapters read with sleepy eyes, the girls climbed into their beds. Michaela wore orange pajama bottoms and a yellow tee shirt. Hayley might have been wearing one of the velour sets of pj's that Megan Alexander gave her each year for Christmas.

Hayley's room was UConn Huskies–blue in color and had that poster of Swin Cash, who is now a beautiful WNBA player, adorning one wall.

Michaela's room, on the other hand, was pastel-bright and a veritable Noah's Ark of stuffed animals. Though cheery and comforting, the room was just Michaela's second-favorite place to sleep. Soon after she'd turned out the light, she slipped from her bed and padded down the hall to the master bedroom, where she climbed into bed with her mother.

CHAPTER TWELVE

Joshua accessed his email and entered his password: 696969. In his inbox was a new email from Caroline, from Arkansas. He clicked on it and then opened the attachment: a new naked photo of her filled the screen. He was instantly aroused. All that time in jail, all those nights when he had only his imagination, had built up in him an insatiable desire. He took himself in his hand and felt his world slip away. Better than jail, but far from the real thing, he thought. Then the phone rang and Caroline's voice became the soundtrack to his fantasy.

Months later, Caroline would tell a reporter that she and Joshua did "talk a bit" about things other than sex. She suspected that he had gone back to robbing houses. But all of that was now inconsequential to the phone- and cyber-sex.

Though the timing isn't completely clear, it was either just before or during the cyber-sex session when Joshua's best friend, Jason, stopped by. Jason had hosted a barbeque on Friday night, hadn't seen Joshua since then and was worried. A front-page *Hartford Courant* article later described Joshua as being despondent, "burying himself in a bottle of whiskey" at the barbecue. The news story pointed to Joshua's broken relationship with Caroline as the motivation to go back to burglarizing houses. "All he talked about was how he was trying to save money so he could pay for her to come back here and then get a place where they could live together," said a friend of Joshua's to the reporter from the *Courant*.

Sure, he was depressed about Caroline moving, Joshua would admit some months later. Though his relationship with Caroline undoubtedly played some role in his mood the night of the barbecue and his actions after, to categorize her leaving as the first domino in some horrible chain of events disregards a criminal nature. The risk of a burglary excited Joshua like a sexual act. It also ignores the influence of a lifetime of cyclical depression.

He had gone to the cookout with a young friend named Nate, the younger brother of a friend of Caroline's and someone with whom Joshua had formed a sort of older, comrade-in-arms role. "I thought I could share my experience with him and spare him from the dark places where I went," Joshua remembered. Joshua was nearing the precipice of one of those dark places at Jason's. And the booze wasn't helping matters.

But that was Friday, and by Sunday he had begun to emerge from his depression. Saturday night with Hayes had stirred his criminal nature. When Jason walked into the bedroom, Joshua closed the laptop and shrugged off his friend's concern. Jason either didn't know or didn't remember about the other renovation job Joshua was doing that had taken up most of his friend's weekend.

Anyway, Jason should've known better than to worry about his pal's whereabouts. Joshua never let anyone know his whole story. The "mystery," he called his illusiveness, or his "smoke and mirror illusion." He only let people know what he wanted them to know. He'd give them part of the truth, but never all of it. He saw this deception as a kind of power—Machiavellian almost.

Joshua told Jason that he was busy getting plans together

to renovate his parents' house, that he'd stopped by Stop & Shop that afternoon to see someone about some money he was owed. He didn't tell Jason about the naked picture on his laptop. He didn't tell Jason about the BB gun or the plastic ties. He didn't tell Jason about the Pacifica he'd followed home. Instead, he said that he couldn't hang out, that he had to see a guy about a contracting job.

Jason said goodbye and told Joshua that they'd meet up during the week. "For sure," his life-long friend said. It was a promise that Joshua wouldn't keep.

CHAPTER THIRTEEN

Dr. Petit grabbed some reports and headed to the couch in the sunroom. He was also dressed in pajamas; the Petits were a pajama type of family. Everyone was in bed and the house again was his own. It was Sunday night, and a busy week—as always—lay ahead. He had left some reading to the last minute.

The sunroom looked out into the backyard, which was guarded by several tall trees. The Petit house sat on a small piece of property on the corner of Sorghum Mill Drive and Hotchkiss Ridge, a tiny road that loops back to Sorghum Mill. Although the Petit property was fairly private, the neighbors' homes, both on Sorghum and Hotchkiss, were only a matter of fifty yards or so from the sunroom.

For certain though, the backyard was quiet while Dr. Petit lay on the couch. Only the summer sounds of crickets and the brush of the pines in the breeze. When it rained, Dr. Petit could hear the drumming of raindrops falling on Michaela's trampoline. The rhythmic sounds, the dry reading, weighed on the doctor's eyelids. And then, as the sound of tar crunching under the tires of a passing car faded into dream, he fell asleep.

CHAPTER FOURTEEN

Alone now in the empty and quiet bedroom, Joshua's immediate surrounding was much the same as when he was a child. But any warm, family feelings this bedroom evoked could be overshadowed in an instant by the memory of what he called his "personal horror show." It was protracted, the sexual abuse, taking place over several months when he was 6 years old and his parents had taken in two foster children, a boy and a girl. The boy became Joshua's persecutor, according to Joshua's parole hearing records. Whether the psychological corruption born from that abuse had any influence with Joshua's criminal behavior or his actions later that Sunday night is pure conjecture. But according to Joshua himself, there were times when he had no control over the demons that roamed his mind.

Joshua pulled his black hooded sweatshirt over his head. Jude Komisarjevsky would later tell the police that her son wearing that sweatshirt gave her a bad feeling. He walked out the door and closed it behind him without saying so much as a word to her.

CHAPTER FIFTEEN

Sometime before midnight, Steven Hayes barreled down Route 8 in his GMC Sierra pickup truck from his mother's house in Winsted to meet Joshua at the Stop & Shop. Hayes might have thought better about speeding. Twice, while on parole, he had been pulled over for moving violations, and twice he was arrested for having drugs or drug paraphernalia in the car.

But if the definition of insanity is doing the same thing over and over and expecting a different result, then Steven Hayes was certifiable. His arrest sheet looks like the "Smith" section of a phone book: every line is just about the same. Twice he was arrested for nearly identical crimes, both times breaking into cars in the same isolated parking lot. Not unusual, perhaps, for a crook as predictable as Hayes. That is until you consider that the two arrests were separated by nine years. As a criminal, Hayes was far from a mastermind. But in a life in which he'd received very few breaks, Hayes had finally gotten lucky.

That he was at this moment behind the wheel of his truck a free man was either a miracle or a testament to the ineptitude of Connecticut's parole system. During his extensive experience in the criminal justice system, one that included arrests in the state of Connecticut for, among other crimes, weapons possession, burglary, larceny and narcotics possession, Hayes had racked up five unsuccessful community releases and had once tried to escape from a halfway house. His last attempt at a community release was also unsuccessful. That one was at Berman Treatment Center.

A seventeen-bed drug rehab for special parolees, Berman is in Bloomfield, Connecticut. It was to Berman that Hayes was sent in June of 2006, and where he first met Joshua. The date that Joshua was transferred to Berman is perhaps significant only in that it began his unholy alliance with Steven Hayes. That date was 6/6/06.

The connection between Hayes and Joshua strengthened further when they both were sent to a work release residence called Silliman House on Retreat Avenue in Hartford. But the budding friendship was interrupted abruptly in November of 2006 when Hayes failed a drug test and was sent back to the Gates Correctional Institution in Niantic, Connecticut.

It is not shocking that Hayes was using drugs. According to the Connecticut Department of Correction, 88 percent of inmates in their system have substance abuse history and a significant need for treatment. Hayes fell squarely inside this demographic. In and out of drug treatment programs his entire adult life—most of it counted behind bars—his criminal history is littered with crimes committed in the pursuit of drugs or when he was high. In jail, he was disciplined no fewer than twenty-three times for transgressions that included intoxication and possession of contraband.

Hayes evinced a character trait common among addicts: the propensity to believe his own lies. There is an old saying heard in Cocaine Anonymous rooms, rooms in which Hayes had often sat: "The definition of an addict is someone who would steal your wallet, then help you look for it."

"I did *not* get high," Hayes wrote in a letter to the parole board in February of 2007 after testing positive for cocaine in Silliman House.

> *"I have been clean in recovery for 47 months, I go to meetings faithfully, I work my steps. I am a member of World Services of Narcotics Anonymous."*

But the official incident report had this to say about Hayes's return to the halfway house:

> Hayes adamantly denied using cocaine so it was tested again, by another staff member with a new test kit. Both times he tested positive. After the test results were shared with Hayes, he became very anxious, pacing around the HWH and ranting foolishly to the point that staff at the House called PO Lindley back and reported that they thought that he was a serious flight risk.

Hayes remained adamant. He wrote to the parole board stating that he was trying to get a hair follicle test, which he insisted would exonerate him. But the letter, like a score of similar ones he had sent over the years he'd been in jail, was really a transparent attempt to get out of jail. He wrote:

> *. . . could it be possible to have my VTP* [voted to parole] *date moved up? I have a sponsor to parole to. My mom. I furloughed to that residence so it's D.O.C.* [Department of Corrections] *approved. I have a job I can return to. I have 47 months drug free. I have many people behind me now for support . . . I have an N.A.* [narcotics anonymous] *support system and I use it. I owe all that is good in my life today to N.A. and living in recovery.*

On April 10, when Joshua was released on parole, Hayes was still in Gates Correctional and had little hope to get out any earlier than what his sentence called for. Then unexpectedly, inexplicably, in May of 2007, he was released on parole. "I don't know why they let me out of jail," Steven Hayes wondered to a halfway house pal. "But I wasn't going to say 'no.'" There is a prison photo taken of Hayes just before his release. In it, he wears an orange prison uniform over a white tee shirt. The top of his bald head barely reaches the 5'6" stripe on the chart behind him. His cheeks rise high from the smile on his lips. Things were finally going Hayes's way.

Upon his release, he almost immediately called Joshua, who was working at the Hartford roofing company. At the time, Joshua's jeans still covered the monitoring device around his ankle.

Aside from having shared the similar experience of all convicts, another reason Joshua forged a friendship with Hayes might have had something to do with a need for approval from older men, whom Joshua had a history of befriending. There was the man I'll call Uncle Joe, a drug-using partner he'd known while living in Southington, and more than several Christian youth pastors and other mentors, including Mark Middlebrooks, a tour director for a Christian performance group who called his relationship with 16-year-old Joshua "profound." Joshua liked to say he was born in the wrong century; "born too late" might have been a better characterization. Joshua called Hayes "Steven," as opposed to Steve, and the proper use of his friend's first name was somehow at once intimate and respectful.

This alliance between Joshua and Hayes began in a law-abiding light. One positive personality trait the two did share was that they both liked to work. And both at first had plans to legally make as much money as they could once they were on the outside. Throughout his work history, albeit one truncated by incarceration, Hayes was a workhorse. As the manager of a thrift store for whom Steven worked wrote:

> *His work ethic was wonderful. [He was] always early, worked everyday, always did his job well above what was expected.*

During his time in Cheshire Correctional, Hayes took advantage of food service courses and learned how to cook. He showed real talent. In one Cheshire Correctional Center "open house," a community relations affair held on prison grounds, Hayes's deviled eggs drew raves. He would go on to work kitchens in two prisons, Enfield and Northeast, where he bragged that he was "the first cook!"

He also had chances to show his talent on the outside. He said he once so impressed a member of Sheryl Crow's road crew at a VIP tent at a Hartford show that he was offered a job as the band's cook. He didn't explain, however, why he didn't take the job. During periods of freedom, he worked in several of the better restaurants in central Connecticut.

Restaurant work, especially kitchen work, is notorious for its long hours. During one work release stint, Hayes took a job in a restaurant called the Chowder Pot in Hartford. Parole records show that he was averaging fifty to sixty hours a week working the kitchen.

Though he worked a variety of jobs, among them at a Salvation Army store, a body shop and as a landscaper—and many times two jobs at once—his dream was to one day run a big-time kitchen in a fancy restaurant.

But the reality of his situation was far less inspiring. Outside of prison walls, hours and hours in furnace-hot kitchens for little pay is what he received for his dreams.

Joshua didn't mind working up a sweat either. But Joshua's plans included more than just putting in as many hours as he could. As the son of an electrician, and having been around tools his whole life, Joshua had the expertise to seriously consider his own contracting business. He liked to brag that he could build an entire house "from laying the foundation to hanging the last door." Sure, he'd have to start out working for someone else to build up a little stake and make contacts. But Joshua was too smart to stay a laborer for long.

It was in the work release residence that Joshua and Hayes began to share their plans. And, later, they would put the plans to practice with a side job or two that Joshua arranged. And though, in hindsight, it is obvious that they brought out the worst in each other, the beginning of the relationship looked like one that would be mutually beneficial. But it is not a stretch to imagine that underneath their hopes and plans roiled a shared simmering anger at their lots in life. For Hayes, who was nearly a lifer behind bars and an admitted crack-cocaine addict, that lot was all that he was denied on the outside: the cars, homes and money. For Joshua, it was something far more psychologically intricate and sinister.

In freedom, it didn't take long for the wall of Hayes's sobriety to begin to crumble—that is, if there was any sobriety to begin with. One of the provisions of Steven's last parole was that he participate in a drug-treatment program run by Catholic Charities. The program dropped him in June 2007 for not attending mandatory meetings. His parole officer was notified. But according to one published report, the parole officer felt that Hayes was doing just fine by holding down two jobs—as a short-order cook and working for a contractor. If that was the case, the parole officer didn't fully comprehend Hayes's drug history. He had violated parole at least twice before, despite the fact that in both instances he was employed full-time. Ask any crack-cocaine addict: in a foot race the urge to get high beats working for a weekly paycheck by the length of the block.

But for a short time, it looked like Joshua and Steven would have a successful—and legal—partnership. They built a backyard deck, and had obtained another client who wanted his garage renovated. But if a seismograph were keeping track of Steven and Joshua's likelihood to commit a crime, it was at this point when the needle spiked off the graph.

Joshua told the Hartford man, Greg Lewis, that the job would cost about $7,000. But a few days later, Joshua tripled the price. Stunned, Lewis turned Joshua and Steven down. Then Steven Hayes's mother, Diana, with whom he lived in Winsted, ordered her son out of the house after she found out that he'd spent several thousand dollars he'd saved to buy a new truck. Diana Hayes had suffered through a number of her son's relapses. Neighbors said that around this time, Mrs. Hayes looked wan and sick. She walked with a cane. Her son's empty bank account, she knew, was a sure sign he was back on drugs, that he had returned to smoking crack-cocaine.

Now Hayes started to become desperate. Staying at his mother's was a provision of his parole agreement. He needed an apartment with a lease right away. He also needed to come up with a fast story as to why he was leaving his mom's or he would be violated back to jail. What he needed was fast money.

In the halfway house, and later working on roofs together, Joshua had regaled Hayes with stories of the cash and prizes of his criminal exploits, like the winning contestant on *The Price is Right*. One story Joshua liked to tell was from the time when he was transporting pounds of marijuana from Vermont to Virginia. One night, he walked into a bedroom where his girlfriend Jennifer slept and dumped the contents of a bursting backpack on her: ten- and twenty-dollar bills. It was stories like that one that would make Hayes's eyes light up. Yes, maybe his new pal could help him out of this jam, he thought.

That's when Hayes went to Joshua with a proposal. And for reasons that will take some explaining, Joshua decided to help him.

The last line in the Connecticut parole agreement that both Joshua and Hayes signed read:

> It is the hope of the Board of Parole in granting you this parole that you will accept it and its conditions as an opportunity to prove to yourself and to others that you are capable of living as a responsible, law-abiding citizen of society and of your community.

Hayes wheeled his pickup into the parking lot and skidded to a stop right next to Joshua, who slowly shook his head. Hayes, no doubt, wore a wide smile. It was at that moment that their signatures on the above document became worthless.

With Hayes riding shotgun, Joshua turned the Venture out onto Route 10 and headed north. Say what you will about the pile of junk he was driving, it certainly didn't draw any suspicion—just another Connecticut soccer mom's van. But in the back of the nondescript vehicle lay his burglar clothing and tools. And there were also zip ties and a modified BB gun, items that he had picked up that afternoon. Joshua had already begun to formulate a crime that was frighteningly more daring than anything he'd attempted.

They headed to the Sports Rock USA in Bristol to have a

few beers and then see what the rest of the night held. Everybody knew the place, a bunch of TVs and plenty of girls. But
the couple of beers tuned into Southern Comfort, straight,
for Joshua, and shots of something else for Hayes. It was just
before closing time at 1 a.m. when they walked, a bit stiff-
legged, out into the night.

The streets of Bristol were quiet and inviting for the mismatched pair of burglars. Joshua wheeled the Venture in and
out of the neighborhoods like a native. No wonder. He'd
lived in Bristol for a while, back in 2001, right in the midst
of his most active period as a burglar. In Bristol, according
to his own account, Joshua burglarized dozens of houses. It
was stolen goods from houses in Bristol that had led to his
arrest. But that was then, and now he had his old confidence
back, a partner and a whole night ahead of him. They rode
around for over an hour. But for some reason—maybe he was
still too high, or more likely thought Hayes was—none of
the houses seemed like good candidates. It was around 2:30
when he decided to head back to Cheshire.

CHAPTER SIXTEEN

Sorghum Mill Drive is a street that is duplicated thousands of times throughout America. A suburban road where families live and grow, where young children run with Harry Potter–laden backpacks to catch the school bus in the morning. The kind of people who live on Sorghum Mill Drive are ones who retire to bed well before midnight—even on the weekend. At three o'clock on Monday morning there is not a whisper here. It is a time when this street is the most vulnerable. The intermittent glow of the street lamps, and an occasional porch light, is the only illumination. Joshua knew the block, of course, and well before following the Pacifica.

When he was just 12 or 13, he would ride his bike at night on a path through the woods. The bicycle path connected North Brooksvale Road with Higgins Road just a few blocks south of Sorghum Mill Drive. On his mountain bike, wearing his army fatigue shirt and with a backpack slung over his shoulder, he could make the trip in ten minutes, tops—it was less than a mile from his parents' house to the Petit home. At 13, he'd initiated a one-kid midnight crime wave that included, by his own estimation, tens of thousands of dollars in vandalism, shooting a pellet gun at cars passing on Route 10, burglarizing hardware and liquor stores, and a dozen houses or more.

"I've hit other sections of Petit family's naborhood many times in '93," he would later write.

As the Venture slowly rolled by the Petit house, Joshua whispered to Hayes, "This is it." Joshua had given Hayes the particulars: the Chrysler Pacifica, the two daughters, and the youthful mother with the blonde hair. Joshua turned off the lights on the van and let it roll to a stop about six or seven houses down from 300 Sorghum Mill Drive. As he stepped from the parked van, the still blackness of the night enveloped him. It was all so familiar. With Hayes trailing behind, Joshua made his way up the driveway.

The only sound in the backyard was from the light rain that fell on the trees and trampoline, a soft glow from the sunroom the only illumination in the otherwise pitch-blackness. Through the windows of the porch, Joshua could see a man lying on a couch, his chest rising and falling with the rhythm of sleep. At first, there was a strange intimacy to Joshua's voyeurism. He intently watched Dr. Petit as if he were trying to figure out what dreams played in the man's head. But curiosity gave way to a surge of power and control. It was in that moment when Joshua decided that it was he, and not Dr. Petit, who would hold dominion over this home. And over everyone who lived under its roof.

He gave the handle of the bulkhead door a gentle tug, and it gave with just the slightest of creaks. Joshua swung open the doors enough to slide into the stairwell and close the door behind him. Joshua owned a small Maglite with tape around the cylinder so he wouldn't chip a tooth if he had to hold it in his mouth. At the bottom of the cement stairs there was a wooden door that led into the basement. This door was locked, but only with a doorknob lock. Child's play for Joshua, who popped it and, just like that, was inside.

He took his time; he always did—at least when he worked

alone. He liked to make himself comfortable and learn the sounds of the house sleeping: the hum of the furnace in the wintertime, the ping of air in the water pipes, the creak of the house settling, the drip of a leaky faucet or the moan of the wind against the eaves. He liked to hear the breathing of those sleeping upstairs.

But on this occasion, Joshua didn't have the luxury of time. Hayes was in the backyard waiting for him, and that made Joshua nervous. Better to get him inside where he could keep an eye on him.

Anyhow, this job was different from all the burglaries he'd committed in the past. From the moment Joshua had bought the zip ties and the BB gun, he'd had something more in mind than just a burglary. It was Hayes's words that had started Joshua formulating his plan. "Would you do an armed robbery?" his partner asked, like a dare. Why not? Joshua had replied. What did Hayes think he was, a punk? But still, Joshua wasn't a convenience-store-holdup–type of guy. And that's when he put it all together. He'd take a family hostage. That would open up all sorts of possibilities, endless possibilities. And he liked the way the younger Petit girl looked.

The beam of the flashlight swept across the basement. Joshua remembers that it was filled with the usual suburban clutter: boxes of Christmas lights and decorations, a washer and dryer, folding chairs and other items stashed or forgotten. But one item drew his attention. It was leaning right at the foot of the staircase that led to the kitchen, just like someone had left it for him. Better than a BB gun, he thought. Joshua grabbed the Louisville Slugger and held it at his side as he silently climbed the stairs.

Hayes stood in the darkness outside the house, his hands in his pocket. How out of place he was: a life-long convict in

the bosom of suburbia in the still of the night. He had children of his own. Two. A boy and a girl. Not that he had ever
been anything like a father to them. In a letter from jail,
Hayes later wrote that his son had had "blackouts," from the
emotion he'd experienced when Hayes tried to reenter his
life and then was sent back to prison. Never did he own a
home, or even have a job for any real length of time. And
now, here he was, standing right in the yard of a family who
represented success in every single thing at which he had so
utterly failed. He thought about Joshua's description of the
family inside. Two kids, just like he had, but here, both girls.
And Joshua had also told him about the tall, blonde-haired
mother. Hayes again shuffled his feet. What the hell was
taking Joshua so long? Hayes muttered to himself.

Silently, and with the confidence of someone who had done
this many times before, Joshua crossed through the kitchen
and into the sunroom. For a moment he stopped in the doorway. The figure on the couch didn't stir. The only sound
coming from him was the rhythm of his breath, the sound of
peaceful sleep. Joshua approached the couch, and as he did,
he raised the baseball bat.

Dr. Petit's head exploded in a bolt of searing white light.
There is not a chance he could have understood what was happening to him. One moment he was sleeping soundly and the
next he was awakened by a pain that felt as if his head were
split in two. In whatever focus he could manage, through pain
and the blood that now gushed from his forehead, was a figure, a man or a boy, with a bat in his hand that he was now
cocking again, and again Dr. Petit's head exploded. Joshua
says he swung the bat as hard as he could—like he was chop-
ping wood.

When Joshua first hit Dr. Petit, he didn't notice Hayes standing outside watching him through the window with this big grin on his face. The audience gave Joshua an added impetus. Again he brought the bat down on Dr. Petit's head. And then again. And again. Joshua would later say that he'd hit Dr. Petit four or five times. There was blood everywhere. But, according to Joshua, as hard as he hit him, Dr. Petit didn't lose consciousness. And that, for Joshua, was just fine. He didn't want any surprises. He knew, of course, that Jennifer, Hayley and Michaela lived under the roof. But he also saw the basketball hoop and the trampoline, and had visions of a tough "17-year-old high school wrestler" sleeping upstairs. Before Joshua climbed those stairs, which he had every intention of doing, he wanted to know exactly what he was walking into, and he wanted Dr. Petit to tell him.

Joshua opened the back door and Hayes was now with him in the sunroom. With zip ties, they secured the doctor's feet, then his hands in front of him. In a voice that was soft and clear, as if he were inquiring about road directions, Joshua asked the doctor to describe the layout of the house, and to tell him who was sleeping and where. According to Joshua, Dr. Petit told him what he wanted to know and then slumped on the couch.

The staircase to the second floor faced the front door. Joshua led the way, his footfalls silent on the carpeted stairs. Gently, he turned the doorknob and pushed open Hayley's door. He remembers that the color scheme of Petit's oldest daughter's bedroom was blue, but he thought it was darker than the "electric blue" described by one of Hayley's friends. He also didn't notice the poster of Swin Cash on the wall. Instead he was focused on the silhouette of the girl sleeping in the bed.

He crept up beside her, with Hayes now in the doorway blocking the little light from the hall.

No one will ever know the thoughts that coursed through Hayley's mind as her eyelids snapped open. Joshua says she didn't scream. But rational thought had to have collapsed into confusion as terror overrode all other brain impulses. How could she possibly understand what was happening to her? She didn't struggle, at least not right away—although out of all the members of the family, it was Hayley who would give him and Hayes the most trouble, Joshua would later say. With Hayes's help, he zip-tied Hayley's hands and fastened her arms and legs to the bedpost with some clothesline they had found in the basement. It was then that Hayley, who Joshua didn't gag, looked at him and asked, "Why are you doing this?" In the same unemotional countenance with which he'd addressed her father, Joshua just smiled.

Quickly, Joshua and Hayes followed the hall to the master bedroom where Michaela slept with her mother. This time, according to Joshua, both he and Hayes went into the room at once. Hayes approached the bed on the side where Jennifer Petit slept, Joshua on Michaela's side. Michaela's eyes opened wide in confusion, but Joshua says she didn't cry. Jennifer too, after a gasp of breath, remarkably held in her emotions, even as they tied her hands, even as Joshua began to lead Michaela out of the room.

It had taken these men fifteen minutes to beat her husband nearly to death and bind and tie her family. Fifteen minutes to turn a family asleep in their own beds into hostages fearing for their lives. But Jennifer Petit's faith in God was matched only by her faith in mankind. Just give them whatever money and things they coveted, she wanted to believe, and they'd be on their way. God would not let anything else happen. How could He? And these two men couldn't be so evil as to want anything else. Jennifer then looked into Joshua's calm, soft eyes. Like countless others throughout his life, she wanted to believe that there was a soul behind them. Please don't hurt my family, Mrs. Petit pleaded. Joshua assured her that the hurting was over.

But it wasn't nearly over.

PART II

CHAPTER SEVENTEEN

The events of July 23, 2007, on Sorghum Mill Drive, sent shock waves throughout Connecticut, indeed the entire country. The crime was the most frightening kind of violation upon the sanctity of our most precious possession: that of a family and a home. The how and why of the crime can be explained straightforwardly as the act of common criminals who exploited the vulnerability of a suburban neighborhood. The Petit family was just the random target of a pair of despicable characters. Joshua was a serial burglar. Hayes was a chronic drug addict who had spent most of his adult life behind bars for crimes committed to support his habit. The combination of the two proved lethal.

But such a quick summation of the Petit case does a disservice to the magnitude of what happened that morning. It leaves out too many important ingredients, indications that perhaps this heinous act was far from spontaneous, but rather was in the making for the lifetimes of the two men accused. Why the Petits paid such a dear price that morning might not ever be fully known. But at least some answers can be found in Hayes's and Joshua's backgrounds.

Almost from the very beginning of his life, Joshua was handed fortunate breaks. He was born on August 10, 1980, in Vernon, Connecticut, and was adopted a few days later.

According to Joshua, his 16-year-old mother had already been pregnant once before and had had an abortion. "She didn't want to go through that again so she gave birth to me and gave me up for adoption," Joshua said. He never pursued tracking down his biological parents: "they left me, I didn't leave them so why would I waste my time reconnecting with someone who didn't want me?" he says. He knew only some bare facts about them, for instance, that his mother was petite and his father, who was 20 when Joshua was born, was tall. "I'm right in the middle—five foot nine," he said (a stretch: police photographs with a height chart background show him to be a hair over five foot seven). He believes that his mother was part American Indian, though this bit of information might only be the wishful thinking of a little boy who loved playing cowboys and Indians on his grandfather's estate. He thinks that his biological parents were drug users. "What else could it have been?" he says with a shrug.

When news stories in the wake of the events that July morning in Cheshire reported the fact that Joshua had been adopted, it stirred up a long-standing debate about "bad DNA" and "criminal genes." There is also a medical belief that a propensity for substance abuse, which Joshua would later exhibit, is inheritable. But ultimately what effect, if any, Joshua's birth parents and their lifestyle had on his life is up for debate. The only thing that is certain is that his adoption would change the direction of his life—and by all early indications, for the better. Joshua had traded up.

Fervent Christians, Ben and Jude Komisarjevsky are by all accounts loving and caring parents. Church members described the Komisarjevskys as a "private" family, and Ben as a quiet man who implements his faith in Christ in all of his affairs. "He was serious about the passions and convictions of what he believed," said Craig Turner, a youth pastor at the Komisarjevskys' church. Joshua is succinct in describing his father: "My father is a devout Christian," he says simply.

An electrical contractor by trade, and an accomplished carpenter, Ben, though from a family of significant wealth, worked with his hands and, by most accounts, was modest and reserved. Unlike his older siblings, who climbed corporate ladders and attained important positions, Ben seemed content with a simple life. Although his father was far from outgoing, Joshua would later say that he has a subtle sense of humor that would often disarm the target of his joke in peals of laughter.

As a librarian in a local grammar school, Joshua's mother was a trained educator. She was fiercely protective of Joshua, but was equally ardent in following the commandments of her faith. Jude would have to choose between the love she had for her son and the rules of her Maker several times in Joshua's life. In those instances, God would usually win. "She'd give me up in a second," Joshua would say with a smile. But those hard choices for Jude wouldn't come until her son entered his teens.

The setting of Joshua's childhood was nothing less than wondrous. He spent the first five years of his life in Torrington, Connecticut. But in 1985, Ben Komisarjevsky moved his family, which now included Joshua's younger adopted sister, Naomi, to Cheshire and into a most interesting living situation.

The Komisarjevskys call their home "the Homestead." The two-story, light gray wooden house on North Brooksvale Road looks, at a quick glance, a bit run-down. The paint on the house is chipped and fading, as is the paint on a wooden wishing well that sits in front. The gravel driveway is rutted and overgrown with weeds. Several cats prowl the property. But considering the structure's age, it's not in bad shape at all. Built in the latter part of the 1700s, the Homestead is part of the estate of John Chamberlain, a noted book critic and author, and Joshua's adoptive grandfather.

The Chamberlain estate encompasses 65 acres of southwestern Cheshire. It is a section of old money, "blue bloods who escaped NYC, Boston, Philadelphia and Los Angeles, but were looking for something different than Greenwich," Joshua once observed. Bordering Chamberlain's property on the southwest is a farm that housed and trained horses for jumping. On the northwest border of the property was another horse farm where they bred, raised and trained Arabian stallions, beautiful horses. As a young boy, Joshua would sneak into the stables in the evening after the hands and trainers had left and feed the stallions apples. In fact, almost every day, the estate would provide Joshua with endless entertainment.

Home from Norton Elementary, the public school just up the street from the Homestead, the precocious boy with the red hair and ears just a bit too large for his head would tear into the house, locate his dog Sam (short for Samantha, a half Husky half German Shepherd mix) and head out into the woods and let his imagination run free. He eschewed television for games of explorer and war (and cowboys and Indians). He would come to know every square foot of his grandfather's land, from the dense cedar groves in the southwestern portion, to the towering oaks that lined North Brooksvale Road, to the climbing vines in the northwest, to the streams and the foothill of Bethany Mountain to the north. By a child's perspective, the estate stretched to the ends of the world and held wonders in every corner.

Joshua's grandparents lived in the northern part of the estate in a building they called "the old barn." Family lore has it that the old barn was once a stop on the Underground Railroad before the Civil War. In the mid-1980s, Joshua's grandfather hired a local architect to design and oversee renovations to the barn that included a dance studio for his wife, Joshua's grandmother, Ernestine, who was a dance teacher.

Not far from the barn is a spring-fed pond with a cement base that once held a diving board. A footpath from the pond leads down a very steep drop-off to an old foundation, all that's left of John Chamberlain's writing studio. In Joshua's youth it was the perfect setting to pretend he was John Wayne in a bombed-out bunker on Iwo Jima or a fort attacked by Apaches.

One of Joshua's favorite destinations on his grandfather's estate was the stables across North Brooksvale Road and behind the old barn. Far from the majesty of the neighboring Arabians, the residents here were closer to the ground: pigmy goats, a whole herd of them. "Just liked them," Joshua says of his grandfather's choice of that particular farm animal, and then, as an afterthought, "He had regular goats, too." There was a summer or two, when Joshua was 5 or 6, when he spent every day at the stables. There he would help feed and tend to the goats. His motivation, however, was more than just his love of the animals.

Liz, the goats' caretaker, was a pretty brunette about 17 years old. "She needed my help," Joshua remembers. "Who else was going to crush the garlic cloves for her (the task she gave me) and mix it into their bowls? Who else would spread the hay in the stalls for the goats to sleep on?" Joshua remembers Liz's trusty 8-track, on which country music played incessantly. Happily he would go about the chores Liz assigned while dutifully listening to her wax on about the finer points of Pac-Man. It was during one of these chats when Joshua confided in Liz that he was going to be a cowboy "when he got a little taller," he said.

Joshua's attachment to Liz, who lived in a house adjacent to the estate, grew even stronger when Jude and Ben hired her as a babysitter. A handful, Joshua had dispatched several of Liz's predecessors. "I was a regular Dennis the Menace," he remembers. But when Liz walked through his front door that first day, all of the practical jokes he had in store for his new babysitter dissolved in her presence. "I was on my best behavior," he says. Alas, nothing lasts forever. And, one late summer day, Liz softly broke the news. She was off to "some far away place called college," Joshua remembers. And Joshua would be off to a place called Norton Elementary School.

It would be at Norton where Joshua's behavioral problems would first surface.

CHAPTER EIGHTEEN

Along with the wonders of the estate, Joshua's adoption brought him a storied lineage and an accomplished extended family. Joshua took plenty of teasing as a child, in school and church, because of his unusual last name, and throughout his life, the pronunciation and spelling of it has been butchered by everyone from police officers to the U.S. Army to newspaper reporters. After that July morning, some newspaper stories about the Cheshire murders would include the phonetic spelling of his name. But long before Joshua attached infamy to it—and the importance of its pronunciation and spelling to law enforcement and the press—the name "Komisarjevsky" was one with a rich history that begins, to no one's surprise, in Russia.

When Joshua was adopted into the Komisarjevsky family, he instantly inherited a Russian grandfather (his grandmother had been married twice) who'd gained fame as a theatrical director. Theodore Komisarjevsky was a product of a show-business family. An opera singer, his father, Fyodor Komisarjevsky, counted Tchaikovsky as a close friend. Theodore's sister, Vera, was an actress of equal or greater fame than their father. But as his adopted grandson would many years later, Theodore wanted to be an architect, and studied the discipline in school. When his sister asked him in 1907 to help stage plays in her theater, however, a dormant devotion bubbled to the surface. In very little time, Theodore gained a reputation as a directing visionary, and actors who learned at his studio had luminous careers on the Russian stage.

For several years, he was the principal director of the Bolshoi Theatre in Moscow. During the Russian Revolution, and Lenin's purge of the arts, Komisarjevsky immigrated to London. Chekhov was his specialty, and in the West End, actors the likes of John Gielgud and Charles Laughton performed for him. During World War II, Komisarjevsky moved again, this time to the United States. It was in New York City where he would notice a beautiful young dancer named Ernestine Stodelle, 31 years his junior.

The romance between Theodore and Ernestine was something of a backstage affair. Komisarjevsky, who had been married before, was engaged to an actress named Peggy Ashcroft when he began dating Ernestine. He would even marry Ashcroft, only to leave her almost immediately and then marry his young dancer.

Theodore and Ernestine had three children, a girl, Tanya, and two boys, Christopher and Benedict, Joshua's adoptive father. The Komisarjevsky family moved from New York City to Darien, Connecticut, where Ernestine started a dance studio. Theodore's death in 1954 (at the age of 72) left Ernestine as a 41-year-old widow with three teenagers. It is at this point that the name "Chamberlain" enters Joshua's lineage.

Considered a "giant" of conservative journalism, John Chamberlain, Sr., once held the influential position of *New York Times* daily book reviewer. But his résumé also included being Henry Luce's editorial page writer at *Life* magazine, a syndicated columnist for Hearst and a framing member of the *National Review* with William F. Buckley, with whom he was friends for forty-five years. In a May 1, 1995, obituary, Buckley wrote this about Chamberlain:

> . . . *the combination of a gentle nature and a hard Yankee mind brought forth prose pure and lasting. His was a voice of reason, from an affable man, unacquainted with affectation, deeply committed to the cause of his country and to liberty.*

Often called "gentle," and "soft-mannered," Chamberlain was a family man who gave priority to skating lessons for his daughters over editorial board meetings.

One of those daughters was Margaret Chamberlain, who happened to be taking dance classes at Ernestine's studio. Margaret's mother (Chamberlain's wife) died the same year as did Theodore Komisarjevsky. After an appropriate period of mourning, Margaret urged her father to give her dance teacher a call. The plan, a long shot by most measures, would pay off with the marriage in 1956 of John Chamberlain and Ernestine Stodelle Komisarjevsky.

By most accounts, the splicing of the Chamberlains and the Komisarjevskys worked out very well. Though it is not known what kind of financial condition Komisarjevsky left his widow in (the director was married multiple times, so one can draw his own conclusions), Ernestine's marriage to Chamberlain solidified her future, and came with an estate in Cheshire. This is not to say she wasn't in love. All indications point to a very happy union. Along with the children from their previous marriages, they would have a child together, John Chamberlain, Jr. And Ernestine and John Chamberlain were married for nearly forty years.

Indications are also that John Chamberlain's love of his wife's children was as robust as that of his own. Before Chamberlain had the old barn renovated, the family lived in the Homestead. Ben, along with Joshua's uncle, Christopher Komisarjevsky, grew up there (it is believed Tanya was already out on her own). In a business management book he wrote with his wife, Reina, Christopher remembered his stepfather fondly. John Chamberlain introduced him to hockey, tennis and writing. And Chamberlain undoubtedly was proud of Christopher's life and career. An Army captain who flew helicopters in Vietnam, Joshua's Uncle Chris had a spectacular rise in business, one that culminated as the CEO of Burson–Marsteller Worldwide, a public relations giant. "My uncle lives in a mansion in a private, gated community on Long Island with their own private beach," Joshua wrote. Chris had nine children from two marriages. The book that he authored, *Peanut Butter and Jelly Management*, draws parallels between parenting and business.

Later in his life, Chamberlain would also take a special interest in his adopted grandson, Joshua. One neighbor remembered Joshua as a tike on a tricycle "tearing up" grandfather's tennis courts—much to Chamberlain's delight, Joshua might add. Chamberlain died in 1994 when Joshua was 14. It was an event, Joshua would later write, that had a profoundly sad effect on him.

Joshua also remembers his grandmother Ernestine as a "poised force to be reckoned with," and "aristocratic." He contends that he was one of her favorite grandchildren, though he admits that some of that had to do with a "close geographical proximity." She had an appreciation, Joshua wrote, for his "social grace," an ability to adapt and interact with people, even those of the rarified dance theater world to which she belonged. But she would also lecture Joshua on what she called his "more delinquent eccentricities." Ernestine died at 95 in January 2008, living long enough to see her grandson accused of capital murder charges.

CHAPTER NINETEEN

If anything, Joshua's adoptive lineage was an advantage rich in history and culture. But his genetic make-up proved in his childhood to be both a hurdle and harbinger of dark things to come. Almost from the start of school, Joshua had trouble in class. It's not clear when exactly he was diagnosed, but according to court records, he was both dyslexic and dysgraphic, a condition with common characteristics such as reversing letters/numbers, writing words backwards, writing letters out of order, and very sloppy handwriting.

Jude Komisarjevsky, Joshua's mother, was the librarian at Norton Elementary, and was able to monitor her son's progress—or lack thereof—in class. Mom Komisarjevsky would tutor Joshua at home. She taught him to spell not by the usual method, or by phonics, but by recognizing the height of the letters. But Joshua's teachers didn't have nearly the patience of his mom. Often the young student got frustrated. In his early school years, Joshua dealt with his frustration with tears and pouting. In fifth grade, tears and pouting became something else.

Joshua had one teacher—an older woman with a dour personality—who went out of her way to humiliate him in class, Joshua says. Rail-thin, she would crook a bony finger and summon him to the front of the room. There she would make him work out a problem on the blackboard that he would most times have no chance of solving.

Along with having a learning disability, Joshua was extremely shy as child. Mentors and Christian youth pastors remembered his reticence. Mark Middlebrooks, a tour director for a Christian performing troupe to which Joshua belonged, recalled his first impression of a young Joshua as "reserved, perhaps even withdrawn." That is, until Joshua was engaged, and then he "came to life." But these feelings of inadequacy combined with his shyness evinced themselves, at least to the teacher, as characteristics of a slacker.

"This is what happens when you don't do your homework," his teacher would announce to the class at Joshua's expense. After several of these demonstrations, Joshua, his cheeks burning red, sulked back to his seat. Just before he arrived at his desk, he grabbed hold of an empty chair and, with all his might, flung it behind him at his teacher.

According to court documents, Joshua was diagnosed with Oppositional Defiance Disorder (O.D.D.). Described in the *Diagnostic and Statistical Manual*, Third Edition (DSM-III, the authoritative reference for psychological abnormality), as a recurring pattern of negative, hostile, disobedient and defiant behavior in a child or adolescent, it is thought to be a fairly common condition that affects somewhere around 10 percent of children. It is also supposed to be contained to a short period of time (a matter of months).

Recent research has uncovered that some youngsters diagnosed with O.D.D. might actually have been bipolar, a label that was then rarely used by the medical community in regards to children. Today, much more is known about childhood bipolar disorder, which was once also described as "manic depression."

In Joshua's case, he would not grow out of his defiant and hostile episodes. Only when he would begin to suffer extended periods of deep depression, an affliction that culminated into a series of suicide attempts in his middle to late teens, is there documentation that the family sought professional help, and did so grudgingly. Joshua's parents put their trust in their own faith in God to help heal their son.

But when Jude Komisarjevsky heard about Joshua acting out in class, she hurried down the hallway to the principal's office. Mom Komisarjevsky knew all about his teacher and Joshua's difficulties with her. Jude didn't like the way the teacher embarrassed her son. At first, she didn't want to intercede on how her co-worker taught class. That was until she saw the frightened look on Joshua's face, and the stern, unyielding countenance of his teacher. "I can teach my son better than she can," Joshua remembers his mother saying to the principal.

Jude grabbed Joshua by the hand and left the office. And Joshua would not attend another public school. This change in the path of his education, however, didn't seem to inhibit his intellectual progress.

Despite his learning disabilities, Joshua's aptitude for accumulating knowledge is extraordinary. His self-professed 150 on the Stanford-Binet I.Q. test would put him well into the genius category. Although proof of the test score has not been made available, Joshua's claim is not far-fetched. Along with the court records that cite his photographic memory, he was also surrounded by wonderful tutelage, the combination of which formed a unique learning experience.

Home-schooled, he flourished as a student. "My mom is a phenomenal teacher," he says. "She'd take me out into the world to learn." Lessons on art would be accompanied by trips to galleries and museums; lessons in the American Revolution would include trips to Boston Harbor and New England Revolutionary battlefields. Mr. Komisarjevsky pitched in by providing hands-on lessons. Joshua learned fractions and calculus from woodshop measurements.

And then there were Joshua's grandparents, whose presence alone was of great influence. Though conservative politically, and a member of the landed gentry, John Chamberlain was something of a Bohemian in nature, and to Joshua he imparted his love of the outdoors, literature and music. Urbane and witty, Ernestine's appreciation for art and fashion too rubbed off on her young grandson. Ernestine often had dance recitals in the old barn's dance studio. To Joshua she would give the job of directing the cars down the long gravel driveway off of North Brooksvale Road. Joshua would show up for the assignment with a ready smile, dressed in his best, with his hair slicked and combed. "You shine up well," Ernestine would tell him.

But there was also some more formal schooling in Joshua's early education. For a while, he attended a Christian school, part of the Association of Classical & Christian Schools (ACCS). Far from the unstructured home-schooling, students in the Christian school were required to wear uniforms not unlike those worn in Catholic schools: the boys in white shirts, ties and navy blue pants, the girls in full-length blue plaid smocks. The manifesto of the organization is Dorothy Sayers's essay "The Lost Tools of Learning," which promotes the idea that the "trivium" of grammar, logic and rhetoric equips students with ability to learn any subject. Courses in Latin and Greek coincide with a reading list that includes the epic poems of Dante and Homer, and the works of Shakespeare. All of the lessons are taught through a Christian worldview. As the Association's mission statement reads:

We recognize that Christ was born in the reign of Cae-
sar Augustus, and that Christianity took root and grew
to maturity in the West. For this reason, we believe
that we must teach certain subjects so that they are
understood and appreciated. This includes ancient history, languages, and culture, studied in the light of biblical Christianity and its impact on western culture.

The combination of his grandparents' influence, his mother's library catalogue and the lesson of the Christian school
provided Joshua with a reading list that rivaled any taught in
the best of prep schools. Along with the works of Shakespeare, including *Macbeth*, *Hamlet*, *The Tempest*, *The Taming
of the Shrew* and *Romeo and Juliet* (the film with Leonardo
DiCaprio among his favorite movies), Joshua studied Ma-
chiavelli's *The Prince*, Plato's *The Republic*, Tolstoy's *War
and Peace*, and Aristotle's *The Poetics* and *The Politics*,
translated by Theodore Buckley and William Ellis respec-
tively; he added Crane's *The Red Badge of Courage*, Aus-
ten's *Pride and Prejudice*, Hugo's *The Hunchback of Notre
Dame*, and, of course, Poe's "The Raven," and many more
classics.

Many years later in his life, while in solitary confinement
in a Connecticut jail, Joshua would write an 11-page letter
describing his love of the Acropolis. In his essay, Joshua
mused about the principal schools of philosophy practiced
there. He compared the Stoics and Epicureans to a modern-
day political debate between right-wing evangelicals and
"some combined effort of hippies, punk and indie rockers,
and protest happy anarchists locked in a small hot room together without water."

The debate in the Acropolis he imagined was also not so
different from the internal tug-of-war with which Joshua

struggled. Throughout his life, Joshua's desire to embrace his Christian surroundings would weaken when confronted with a craving to do just the opposite. A normal internal conflict for many, but in Joshua this struggle would begin to show itself in increasingly dramatic ways. Joshua himself would call it his personal civil war, "battling on the grounds of my soul."

Though homeschooling and the strict environment of Christian school managed to keep Joshua's behavioral problems confined, there is no evidence that anything was being done to address them in a professional or clinical way. And when Joshua was away from the above constraints, those problems would "raise their ugly head," as he described. A good deal of Joshua's social and sporting activities were conducted in various youth groups attached to the churches (there were several) to which the Komisarjevskys belonged. Joshua was either removed by his parents or asked to leave these groups, "more times than I can count," he says.

Time after time, Ben and Jude would find themselves fending off the complaints of other parents, church leaders and administrators. The family was dismissed from a church group in New Hampshire, near the Komisarjevskys' summer cottage in Alton Bay. By letter, they were informed that Joshua wasn't welcome back the following season, and neither was his family.

All these years later, emotions still run hot. A youth pastor who refused to be interviewed did briefly describe the heartache he continues to have when he thinks back to the raw feelings of that period. The last time he saw Joshua is an image burned into his memory. Wearing his usual skateboarder outfit, Joshua was walking away from the pastor down a lonely road.

Though church members are understandably reluctant to talk about Joshua, in retrospect Joshua himself sees his time as a young Christian with apathy and distrust, writing:

I've never cared much about the religious dogma I'd been taught as a child. I've always been quite willing to ignore injunctions about chastity, righteousness and obedience uttered in church and mostly paid lip-service to by church goers: I'm not, by any stretch of the imagination, a saint.

When Joshua was 9 or 10, he joined the Christian Brigade, a sort of Christian Boy Scouts. Joshua's father, Ben, was a member in his youth. Each summer Joshua would attend a camp run by the Brigade in Kezar Lake, Maine. In the main building of the camp, once a lodge owned by the Roaring Twenties singer Rudy Vallee, hangs the Christian Brigade's motto: "Bright and Keen for Christ."

The group to which Joshua belonged was part of the Cheshire Baptist Church, a non-denominational, evangelical Christian church right on Main Street in Cheshire. In the early 1990s, when Joshua was most involved in the Brigade, the church had a congregation of about 250. Similar to the mission of the Boy Scouts, the Brigade sought to teach character. There were games of skill and skill development. The kids also learned to tie knots and build birdhouses. And, as in the Boy Scouts, the Brigade members could win merit badges. The only difference was, the Brigade taught their lessons through a biblical perspective.

Craig Turner worked for the town of Cheshire back then, as the coordinator of youth activities. He also volunteered at the Baptist church working with the Brigade. He remembers that Joshua stood out from the group, numbering fifteen or so kids at the time, for two reasons. "He was extremely active," Turner remembers. "And easily distracted." The example Turner remembers was when the Brigaders were playing in the gym and break times would come. While the rest of the kids would sit for snacks or water, Joshua would continue whatever activity they had engaged in, like kickball for example. "He kind of liked to do his own thing," Turner says. "And had to be reined in periodically."

Turner describes Joshua from that time as "skinny," "gawky" and "not extremely coordinated." (Joshua contradicts this in a letter he'd write years later where he described himself as "quite" a soccer player in his teens. "I have all sorts of trophies and medals for my abilities," he wrote.) Joshua, according to Turner, got along with some of the other children, but alienated many others. In one way, he was ringleader, always trying to engage other children. Some of them followed. Even as an adult, Joshua took pride in the way he could motivate workers in his contracting crew.

Ultimately, in remembering Joshua from that time, Turner didn't think he was remarkable in any way. "He did not stand out from his peers as being odd or different or weird," he says. But Turner does remember that Ben Komisarjevsky had real concerns about his son. Joshua's father wasn't sure that his son had the constitution—or faith—to overcome his personality problems. Ben was worried about Joshua "just making it," Turner said.

Many years later, in a jailhouse interview, Joshua was reluctant to talk about his relationship with his father, other than to say that both of his parents tried their best with him and that he had put them through more than anyone deserved. Yet, between the few words Joshua did say about him, one had the feeling that Ben was very stern with Joshua and felt a certain amount of frustration over being unable to control his son.

But Joshua's father also went to great lengths to keep the boy entertained. Just about every weekend in the winter, Ben would take Joshua and his best friend, Jason, skiing in Otis, Massachusetts. For Ben and Jude, keeping Joshua busy was a full-time job.

The Komisarjevskys went on summer vacations to Pennsylvania; Wells, Maine; Six Flags New England; the battlefields of the Civil War, Ben & Jerry's Ice Cream Factory in Stowe Vermont; sailing on Lake Champlain; and the White Mountains and Lakes Region in New Hampshire. Joshua remembers family trips to the Berkshires, the Adirondack Mountains and Tanglewood, where he saw Johnny Cash and other concerts. ". . . At night the symphony would continue to play under a fireworks display as us kids played and ran around thousands of blanket islands cast over a sea of grass," he remembers.

Mom Komisarjevsky, with an eye always on Joshua's studies, insisted on trips to Washington, D.C. Vacations to the capital would include a side trip to Chesapeake Bay, where his Aunt Tanya had a home. "My family has taken me to so many places I couldn't remember all of them if my life depended on it," Joshua would write.

But even considering his parents' dedication, Joshua still had plenty of time in which he was left on his own. He also had a 65-acre estate in which to disappear from his parents' control. It was during this alone time in the woods when Joshua would start heading for trouble.

CHAPTER TWENTY

In spite of countrywide economic upturn, Connecticut of the early '90s was still languishing in the recession. Though Big Insurance stayed steady through the uncertain times, the defense industry, the state's other major employer, was struggling. In Cheshire, like in any small town, there was an element of teenage malaise. Nowhere was this more in evidence than with Joshua Komisarjevsky. The 14-year-old would battle his boredom in a criminal and most spectacular way.

Though far from immune from crime—the gang-controlled drug distribution was just a thirty-minute drive away in Hartford—Cheshire in the mid-1990s still had the attributes of a small town, with small-town attitudes. And a small-town stigma was attached to Joshua for setting the fire—there are townspeople who still talk about the blaze all these years later.

Maybe it was because the Huxley garage was something of a landmark in Cheshire. A monument to the days of Ford Pintos and gas rationing, it had lain empty for a number of years and weeds grew high through the cracks of the cement in the parking lot.

Along with being a garage, with several bays and doors, it was also a car dealership with a showroom. But by the mid-1990s it was a town eyesore and a clubhouse for some of Cheshire's budding delinquents, Joshua among them. "There was a lot of beer drinking and other juvenile stuff," Joshua remembers. Mostly it was a nighttime hangout, furnished with old couches and chairs, music provided by a boom box.

The fire started, Joshua says, by accident. And since he was the only one in the garage at the time, there is no way to contradict his version.

It was about noon, he remembers, well before any of his pals arrived. Most of those pals went to traditional schools with traditional hours. Bored and alone, Joshua began flicking matches to pass the time. One of the matches landed on a couch that was soon smoldering. Joshua sat placidly and watched as the couch was consumed. Soon the flames jumped to the oily floor and Joshua calmly made his way out of the garage and to a safe vantage from which he could watch the show.

From across the street, Joshua watched the fire with eyes wide in amazement. In his brown irises the refection of the flames danced and leaped. Deep within, he felt a puckering excitement. Joshua loved fire, loved that it had a life of its own, that it took what it wanted without conscience. Something of a crowd had gathered around him to watch the blaze as it grew to four alarms. Route 10 was jammed with fire trucks that shot arcs of water through the air. The smoke was thick and dark as coal.

Though it would be difficult to find someone to admit this, Joshua's actions solved a long-standing problem. It seems that the immediate area surrounding the garage was up for a historical registration. An editorial in *The Cheshire Herald*, the town's weekly newspaper, had, some months before, called for the garage to be demolished:

Long regarded as the epitome of an eyesore, one of the few situated in a town where architectural attraction is at the forefront of concern.

But the owner of the garage had balked because of the prohibitive cost of an environmental cleanup. The blaze was a quick fix, and undoubtedly a boon for neighboring real estate prices. For Joshua, it was simply spectacular. But at some point, as he sat on his mountain bike, the gas station now a pile of glowing cinder, he started to get paranoid. He had a feeling that the cops knew that he was the arsonist. He wasn't crazy. When Joshua was spotted watching the fire on a security camera tape, he was targeted immediately as a prime suspect. By then, the Cheshire P.D. was very familiar with Joshua Komisarjevsky.

It was two years before the fire when Joshua's criminal career had begun, a day or two before the Fourth of July in the summer of 1992. As early as the previous summer, Joshua had taken to wandering around his grandfather's estate at night. He would wait for his parents to fall asleep, then climb out the window of his bedroom, scamper across the roof and jump out into the backyard flower garden.

As it had when he was climbing the towering oaks, practice emboldened him. By the time he was 12, his nocturnal wanderings had taken him into the neighboring woods, streets and parks of Cheshire. "The night has no boundaries," he wrote, "it offers endless mysteries, discoveries, wonders, and opportunities for fun."

His nighttime hikes went on undetected for months. As long as he got home before his parents awoke, no one was the wiser. But one night he lost track of time. When he saw the first light of dawn, he knew he was in trouble.

Clear across town, he began to race through backyards and down sleepy streets. It was on one of those blocks where he passed a house with a Honda parked in an open garage. Joshua already knew how to drive—he'd driven his father's station wagon when Ben was building a new house on the Chamberlain property.

"I got to thinking that if the family was like everyone I know, the keys would be hanging on a key hook just inside the door leading from the garage to the house," he remembers. Just as he thought, as he cracked open the unlocked door, he saw a set of car keys hanging on a hook. But something else caught his eye inside the house. A pocketbook lay on a counter within reach.

His first crime netted him $80 and a stolen car. He used the car only to get home in time, and left it some distance down North Brooksvale Road.

He used much of the money for fireworks. He and his pal Jay spent the following afternoon shooting off bottle rockets in a field on the Chamberlain estate. It was during that Fourth of July celebration when Joshua the criminal was born.

In the beginning of his criminal career, Joshua's hunting grounds were his hometown. It began almost like a young boy's game. Invisible in his camouflage jacket and black ski hat, he would ride his bike down the dark streets and cul-de-sacs of Cheshire. The woods of his grandfather's estate were the staging area for his sorties, and his sanctuary on his return. He looked for houses that offered easy access: open garages and screen porch doors.

At first, he mostly took cash, stolen from pocketbooks and wallets, and whatever valuables he could stash in his pockets. But as he became more brazen, he'd steal VCRs and camcorders. And the more he broke into houses, the easier it became for him. He started to look for challenges, the larger, more expensive homes, even those with lights burning in upstairs windows.

Early on, he burglarized a local hardware store, where he stole gloves, flashlights, batteries, knives, pepper spray, spray paint and other tools for his new trade. When he saw the key-copying machine, an idea was born. He would break into the hardware store several more times, but only to make copies of house keys he had stolen.

By 1994, Joshua says, he was breaking into an average of eight houses a week in Cheshire and he entered hundreds of houses during this time, including several in the neighborhood of Sorghum Mill Drive. In many of these burglaries, he didn't take a thing. He would sit in dark living rooms and kitchens, and just listen to the sounds of the house. It was this curious habit, and the fact that he broke into houses at night when people were home, that separated Joshua from your average house burglar. It also raises questions of his real motive.

As his pubescent hormones raged, there was something sexual about the act of burglarizing houses for Joshua, something as naughty as it was illegal. According to a retired Cheshire cop, an example of Joshua's hidden motive concerned a family who lived in a house in Josh's neighborhood. More than once, the girl, about Joshua's age, complained to her parents that Joshua was in their yard and looking in her window. One morning she awoke with the feeling that someone had been in her room. The brazenness of such an act seemed impossible. But when some of her personal items were missing, she was convinced.

The violation left the girl in a state of fear. She didn't even like to be alone in the house during the daytime, which is what happened a few evenings later when her parents went out to a Cub Scout meeting. Her fear was realized when she looked out her bedroom window and Joshua stared back. She ran to the phone and called a friend of her family's, a Cheshire police officer. The cop hurried over and knocked on the Komisarjevskys' door. After the officer's visit, the incidents stopped. But as long as Joshua lived next door, the girl never felt completely safe again.

Joshua disputes the above story, dismissing his neighbor as "crazy." But why, as Joshua would admit he did, would someone break into a house, stay there for hours, and steal nothing? It leaves one to wonder whether the seed of what would happen years later on Sorghum Mill Drive had taken root in Joshua's teens.

For certain, there were other emotional triggers that had a part in Joshua's early criminal exploits. One was the death of his grandfather. Joshua remembers that Main Street was blocked off for John Chamberlain's funeral mass held at the First Congregational Church in 1994. To this day Joshua has trouble putting into words his feelings about his grandfather's passing. For months while Chamberlain died a slow death, Joshua held vigil. In a letter from jail, he called Chamberlain, "one of the most pervasively inspiring role models of my life."

More death was brought into Joshua's life in 1994. A fellow by the name of Carr from whom Joshua took drumming lessons died suddenly, and a youth pastor named Chandler, whom Joshua referred to as "his mentor," died of a heart attack in his 40s. In Joshua's eyes, Chandler was not like the other youth pastors and pontificators he encountered in his Christian life. "He wasn't a phony," Joshua said. "You knew when he talked to you that he really cared."

Joshua would later say that he stopped caring after his grandfather's death. He didn't care what the Church said, he didn't care what people thought, didn't even care if he lived or died. But even a freshman psych student would tell you that Joshua's actions were all about caring what people thought, having people notice him. Later, in jail, Joshua would be diagnosed with Antisocial Personality Disorder and severe depression, and score high in traits of schizophrenia. Though the pain of losing his grandfather, Chandler and Carr exacerbated an already delicate emotional balance, the most traumatic event in Joshua's life had occurred many years before. And it took place in his own bedroom.

Perhaps as a compensation for the absence of biological offspring, but more likely as an extension of their enthusiastic faith, Ben and Jude opened their home to two foster children, a boy and a girl. The boy, a young teen, shared a bedroom with Joshua. At the time, Joshua was 6 years old.

Joshua offers few tangible details about the ordeal. The abuse is mentioned only briefly in court records. Joshua's family has declined to talk. But the one thing that is clear is how Joshua categorizes what happened to him. He says that he was not molested, that there was no coaxing or fondling or flashing or other traditional characteristics of a child molester. Instead what he suffered was "forced, merciless rape," and his "personal hell" went unnoticed for months. According to Joshua, the abuse stopped only when the boy's aggression showed itself in more obvious ways to another family member.

Today, when Joshua talks about that time, his eyes get hard and his speech cryptic. He is far more eloquent when he writes about the person he calls his "dictator" and "tyrant." Below is an excerpt from a letter Joshua wrote in jail, months after that July morning in Cheshire:

This child raped of his innocence, guilty of silence, dripping in sin, learned at an early age the art of repression. This terrible feeling grew. In time it became an unconscious raw tingling that jangled my nerve and made me want to jump out of my skin. Rebuke the devil and pray I was told.

Growing up, kids are propped up with lies and promises made with good intentions; life is good, humanity is kind, God is loving . . . But I know, I knew full well that life was a battle, humanity is cruel, and that God is all knowing, all powerful and did nothing to protect this child.

CHAPTER TWENTY-ONE

Despite the biblical lessons imposed upon him by Church and family, Joshua, at 14, was either defiant or incapable of realizing that his criminal actions had consequences. Before his 14th year was over, however, Joshua would have to face reality. That year, for the first of many subsequent times, cops and courts became part of Joshua's life.

He heard the gravel in the driveway crunch under the tires of the car. His throat closed as he parted the curtain in his bedroom window and saw the unmarked police car in the driveway. From downstairs came muffled voices. He stood near his bedroom door trying to hear what they were saying. When his father finally called him down, he tried to act nonchalant. The two detectives sat in chairs facing his parents, who sat on the couch. His father wore a solemn expression, Joshua remembers. His mother was in tears. He thought the cops were there because of the burglaries he'd committed. When they started grilling him about the fire, Joshua was shocked. "The four of them made short work of me," he would later write. "It was probably a Cheshire P.D. record for obtaining a confession."

Joshua started to cry when the detective told him he had to accompany them to the police station. It was then he asked for permission to use the bathroom. As it happened, the bathroom on the first floor of the Komisarjevsky home was being renovated. Joshua climbed the stairs, opened and closed the upstairs bathroom door as he walked by it, and hurried to his bedroom. There he filled a backpack with anything he could grab: some clothing, a hunting knife and a "survival pack" that he had from camp. He took some cash he had hidden in the room, money he'd stolen from the houses he'd burglarized, and stuffed it in his pocket. Before anyone downstairs became suspicious, he was out his bedroom window, and onto the pitched roof. He jumped into the back yard and crossed North Brooksvale into woods behind his grandparents' house. "I knew once I hit the tree line you didn't have a chance in hell of catching me," he wrote.

Joshua says that he spent a couple of days and nights in the woods of his grandfather's estate. During this time, he broke into several more houses, stealing food, cigarettes, money and beer. He took a steak out of one house and cooked it on a grill he'd stolen out of the backyard of another. One night, he took an SUV from a driveway and drove around Cheshire picking up friends and hotrodding. It was when he went to visit a girl named Holly that his escape came to an end. There are conflicting versions, however, of how he was caught.

He began that evening by drinking beer he'd stolen out of a garage refrigerator. By his own admission, Joshua gets depressed when he drinks. "I'm the complete opposite of those who get rowdy, wild and loud," he wrote. It was while he was drinking that he carved the word HATE, along with other long gashes, into his arm with the hunting knife. Drunk now, his arm dripping and sticky with blood, he crossed through the woods to Holly's. When he arrived, a Cheshire police cruiser was parked in front of the house. The cop saw Joshua and a chase ensued, one that Joshua says ultimately included a dozen cops, a half-dozen police cars, being clipped by a police cruiser, and finally brought down by "a flying tackle."

But a lawyer who represented Joshua said that the police found him drunk and asleep next to a bicycle.

Whichever version is true, what is certain is that police brought Joshua to St. Mary's Hospital in Waterbury for medical treatment and a psychiatric evaluation. Thirteen years later, Dr. Petit would be brought to the same hospital.

Joshua's lawyer also said that his client had written a suicide note. The hospital took the note and his carved arm very seriously. He was sedated to the point of unconsciousness. When he came to, he was lying on a hospital bed, his hands and feet in restraints. Upon opening his eyes, the first face he saw belonged to his mother, her eyes welling with tears.

Joshua was transferred to a psychiatric hospital in Portland, Connecticut. Actually, the transfer didn't go that smoothly. The doctor couldn't find the keys to the small padlocks that held Joshua's restraints. With his teeth, Joshua was able to loosen one strap enough to slide his hand out. "The jaws on the officer and doctor dropped and my mom just laughed," he wrote.

No longer called "Elmcrest," the hospital to which Joshua was sent is a private psychiatric facility that is now run by St. Francis Care out of Hartford. According to the St. Francis Care website, the facility offers a "full range of mental health and substance abuse treatment programs for all ages." Joshua, like most of the teenagers he was housed with, was being treated for manic depression. Joshua remembers his psychiatric hospital stay fondly. The building he was housed in was co-ed, he said, his fellow patients between the ages of 13 and 15.

"Something was always happening day or night," he wrote. "We were all emotionally volatile, quick to act up, and not caring about much but the moment." Joshua didn't like any of the boys, calling them "wimpy" and "whinny," [sic] but says he got along with the girls just fine. "I was a rooster in a hen-house!" he wrote. The way Joshua describes his stay at Elmcrest is like some kind of combination of *Fast Times at Ridgemont High*, and *One Flew Over the Cuckoo's Nest*. It was entertaining, Joshua wrote:

> *we didn't have anything better to do than to raise hell and fuck each other brains out in the bathrooms, bedrooms and closets. You would think psychologist and psychiatrist would know better than to house troubled, sexually active teenage rebels into a co-ed dorm . . . not that I was complaining* ☺.

But the 14-year-old's stay at the hospital was far from all fun and games. By his own admission, Joshua was hostile to the orderlies and his rebellion would often find him restrained and in a padded room. Patients and staff alike called it "the blue room," because the floor, walls and ceiling were covered with blue Ensolite mats, the same ones "you find in school gyms across America," Joshua relates. His description of the room includes a "blue-tinted bubble sun window" in the center of the ceiling, and a Plexiglas window in the door ("you felt like a fish in an aquarium," he wrote). The temperature, provided by central air-conditioning, was kept quite cool.

The room contained what Joshua called "the burrito"—a restraining device like a large straitjacket, made up of a canvas sheet and buckles, "but worse because you couldn't even walk," he adds. Joshua writes about being tackled and wrestled into the burrito, and receiving a punch to the face after he was buckled in. His story is not far-fetched. A few years after his stay, the state of Connecticut found Elmcrest negligent in staff training after an 11-year-old boy suffocated while being restrained by an orderly. But Joshua contends that he gave the staff as many bruises as they administered to him.

One day he managed to escape out of the burrito by emulating Houdini while the orderlies applied the restraint. "I surreptitiously took a big breath and held it filling my lungs and puffing out my chest," he wrote. After he heard the bolt lock on the door, he exhaled and had just a slight amount of wiggle room. It took him twenty minutes, but he was able to work himself free. "Boy did that sadistic orderly have a surprise when he came back an hour later to get me." As soon as Joshua heard the bolt slide open, he jumped up and body-slammed the door. The impact of the door was so powerful, Joshua says, that it not only broke the orderly's nose, but both of his eyes were blackened.

It was while at Elmcest that Joshua would first be prescribed anti-depressants and other medication for his emotional problems. Though clinicians believed the medication would help him, his parents, it seems, thought otherwise. For the Komisarjevskys, Jesus Christ was the answer to their son's problems. Moreover, they knew the perfect place to send Joshua for him to improve his relationship with his Savior. And for a short time, after his release from Elmcrest, it looked as though Joshua had found the light.

CHAPTER TWENTY-TWO

Flying down the gravel road, the now 15-year-old with the multicolored hair pedaled furiously. He loved to ride his mountain bike. He especially liked the way the deep treaded tires bit into the soft dirt on the road's shoulders, kicking it up behind him. He liked the way his eyes would tear as he tore through the wind. He was wild on that bike, always just barely in control, always being chastised by the camp director's wife. "You know better, Josh," she would say. With his purple, floppy hair and baggy jeans, in the back pocket of which was a thick wallet held to his belt loop by a chain, Joshua would fashion a sheepish grin in return. The grin, the outfit and the kid were hard to dislike.

The gravel road connected the lakeside camp to the town of Lovell, Maine. Joshua could've done the trip blindfolded. He was a crusty veteran of the Frontier Camp on Kezar Lake, having spent several of the previous summers there at a Bible study. But this trip to Kezar was not voluntary. "I was kidnapped by my own family," he wrote, adding a smiley face to the sentence. Although the court records are sealed, Joshua contends that his extended stay at the camp was a provision of the deal his parents and lawyer made with the court after the Huxley fire. The camp was also Ben and Jude's answer to Elmcrest and anti-depressants.

On the surface, at least, Joshua doesn't hold any animosity towards Ben and Jude. He would later write:

> *As for my parents, they've gone above and beyond trying to give me every possible opportunity to not only succeed and excel in life but to be at peace with myself. The sacrifices they've made personally, financially and emotionally are outstandingly remarkable, if there was a Silver Star and Purple Heart for parenting they deserve several! I'd be devastated and heart-broken to go through with my daughter what I've put my parents through. My choices and subsequent lifestyle in no way reflects the parenting, unconditional love and support they've shown me and amazingly still do. They don't love the actions of their son but do the son himself.*

In the above letter, Joshua went on to say that much more accurate example of Jude and Ben's parenting is reflected in the "silent strength and poise," of his younger sister, Naomi. But Joshua says that he too had "his moments to shine." It was during this camp stay when Joshua would show an inclination to shine, and it would be a girl who would bring out his better side.

Back on the backwoods road, Joshua was going full tilt and was almost to the front gate when he saw the blue van pull in. It wasn't so much the van that caught his attention. In the back seat was a blonde-haired girl about his age who, he could swear, was looking at him! As the van rolled by, the young lady's head swiveled just a bit, and for a moment, Joshua recalls, their gazes locked. As Joshua watched the back of the van bounce and waddle down the gravel road, he couldn't stop thinking about how pretty the girl was.

Fifteen or so minutes later, Joshua was headed back to the main camp building. Pine trees, 120 feet and more high, lined the gravel road. It was late afternoon, and the sun that peeked through the soaring canopy cast a giant jigsaw of shadow. Joshua had to be back to help out with dinner preparation. Kitchen duty was one of the many jobs he performed at the camp. Most of the guests and all of the staff knew Joshua well, and liked him. When he slid to a stop in front of the administrations building, causing a spray of gravel as he did, the blue van was parked in front. A friend with whom he worked in the kitchen was standing on the porch of the building, a dishtowel hung over his shoulder.

"Who's the new family?" Joshua asked, a sideways tilt of his head indicating the van.

"Some pastor from Connecticut," came the reply.

"CT? No kidding," Josh mused. "It's a small world."

As dinner was served, Joshua stood by the kitchen door and watched as the camp director introduced Reverend Mesel. The Connecticut pastor offered grace. Joshua bowed his head and whispered along with the prayer.

While the pastor finished his benediction, Joshua craned his neck for another look at his daughter and was disappointed when she was no longer seated with her family. When dinner was finished, Joshua helped clear and wipe the tables, as usual. The chore helped keep his mind off the girl, and by the time he had poured himself a hot chocolate, he'd all but forgotten her. That is, until he saw her walking down the main staircase, flanked by her two younger sisters.

She was even prettier than he'd remembered, more like beautiful he would later say. Standing there wearing his kitchen apron, soaked in dishwater, Joshua was torn between

A Cheshire firefighter walks past a smashed Cheshire police car at the corner of Sorghum Mill Drive and Burrage Court. The suspects, driving the Petit family Chrysler, reportedly hit three cruisers as they fled.

The Petit house ablaze. Photo taken after suspects fled the burning home. *Alyssa Russell*

Joshua Komisarjevsky's mug shot, taken after his arrest for the events in Cheshire, July 23rd, 2007.

Connecticut State Police

Steven Hayes's mug shot.

Connecticut State Police

A scarred Dr. William Petit standing among mourners at a memorial service for his family.

Alyssa Russell

Firemen investigate a burned area of the home of Dr. William Petit in Cheshire, Connecticut.

AP Photo/George Ruhe

Caroline Mesel, Joshua Komisarjevsky's ex-girl-friend, is seen in Rogers, Arkansas. Mesel talked to Komisarjevsky on the phone just hours before the murders in Cheshire.

AP Photo/Beth Hall

Petit family members arrive at Superior Court in New Haven, Connecticut to see Joshua Komisarjevsky and Steven Hayes arraigned on multiple charges in connection with the deaths of Michaela, Hayley and Jennifer Hawke-Petit.

AP Photo/Bob Child

Dr. Petit at the GE 5K Petit Family Foundation Road Race, a charitable event named after his family.

AP Photo/Jessica Hill

Dr. Petit faces the haunting photo of his dead daughter, Hayley, at a memorial service held at Central Connecticut State University.

Neighbors plant a heart-shaped memorial garden on the plot where the Petit house once stood.

Dr. Petit cannot control his grief at a memorial service at Cheshire High School for his wife and two daughters.

AP Photo/Fred Beckham

trying to make himself invisible and getting up the nerve to talk to her. While the internal tug-of-war was taking place, she marched right over to him.

"Hey, kitchen boy," said the pretty blonde girl unhesitatingly, "I'm Claire."

Whatever courage Joshua managed to muster drained from him like the dishwater in the sink from which he'd just pulled the stopper. Later, on the way to the campfire Bible study out on the point, he was barely able to mumble a sentence to Claire. But by the time the campfire started to die, a teen romance had begun to kindle, one that would last until the next summer or so, an eternity for 15- and 16-year-olds.

Joshua remembers mornings at the camp, sitting on dew-covered grass, watching the waves lap against the rocky shore. He would hear her before he saw her, the flop of her sandals against her bare feet as she approached from behind. "Good morning, sunshine," she would say. Joshua would whisper the same words into Jayda's ear when his daughter would awaken ten years later.

As is the case with many teen crushes, the relationship morphed into a friendship. Claire's father, Reverend Mesel, however, wasn't as malleable. Although Joshua calls the pastor "a good guy," who liked to play basketball and shared his love of Mountain Dew, the feelings did not stay mutual. The reverend wasn't at all happy with the way the young man with the crazy hair had broken his daughter's heart.

At least that's Joshua's version of the story. Joshua would later say that his friendship with Claire was one of the most meaningful he ever had. It lasted until 2007, when Claire found out that Joshua was dating her younger sister—Caroline, Joshua's last girlfriend.

But that relationship was years and a jail sentence away. It's unclear what happened to Joshua's inclination for crime at this point. He does write of being "restless" during this time of his life. But it seems as though the urge to break into houses, at least, had receded.

Part of Joshua wanted to live a life of which to be proud. When Joshua was good, good things seemed to happen to him. Pastors, mentors and friends would go to great lengths to help him. And Joshua truly wanted to justify their faith in him. But through even the happiest times, there existed in Joshua a voice that directed him away from all that was good. That voice would be especially persuasive when Joshua tried to do what was right. When things looked hopeful, he wrote, he battled "the inner struggle that always rage within."

Still, as he turned 17, a unique opportunity arose that gave Joshua a chance to witness first-hand how fulfilling a life lived in God's light could be. And, for a while, it seemed as though Joshua had extinguished for good those disquieting thoughts that roamed his mind.

CHAPTER TWENTY-THREE

Though tales of the Cheshire Correctional Center had no doubt frightened Joshua too as a child, he would not see the inside of that prison, at least not as a juvenile in the John R. Manson Youth Institution. But Joshua's banishment to Frontier Camp had not completely satisfied his legal difficulties. He still faced punishment for the Huxley fire, and the burglaries. Instead of jail time, jurisprudence would decide that the 17-year-old had a soul worth saving, and the court's order would propel the troubled youth into a most amazing journey.

Mark Middlebrooks was an actor and singer with a career in musical theater. At the time he met Joshua, in 1997, Mr. Middlebrooks was a tour director for the Continentals, a Christian performance group that toured the U.S. and Europe.

"I received a phone call regarding a young man in need of focus and direction," he remembered. "I was asked if I would take a chance on him and invite him to join our group. I agreed." The Continentals' mission, according to its website, is "To advance the kingdom of Jesus Christ around the world through music missions, leadership development and performing arts' ministries." That Joshua was accepted into the Continentals surprised even his parents. "We weren't sure if we should believe it or not," Jude Komisarjevsky remembered to a friend.

According to Joshua, the touring group is "fairly selective," in accepting membership. The program is primarily for teens and younger adults. Letters of recommendation from church pastors and youth leaders are required. And then you have to be talented. Although Joshua wasn't applying for a performing position ("you'd think I'd make an excellent cast member with my ability to play role's," he once wrote, "but alas I'm horrible on the theatrical stage! ☺"), his technical background was scrutinized. Even at 17, he had plenty of experience working with tools. In the end, Joshua was accepted by the group, and thereby sidestepped any jail time, because of Mark Middlebrooks. "Having been somewhat troubled myself as a young man, I am eager to provide guidance and support to those who are struggling," he would later say in remembering that time.

Joshua flew out to Santa Barbara where he joined up with the troupe. He was given only a week-long orientation, marathon sessions that went from early mornings to late night. He learned cues, lines and music equipment. And the pressure was on. ". . . if you can't cut it you won't make it on the road and your replaced by the many who want to try," he recounts.

Middlebrooks remembers an eager young man who desperately wanted to succeed and please. "I would never, in a million years have guessed that Josh had ever had any trouble whatsoever, and in fact, quite the opposite," said Middlebrooks. The tour director came to rely on Joshua more and more as the tour took to the road. He described his assistant as the "MacGyver" of the company: ". . . he could take a tin can, a candle, and some duct tape, and light up our stage like a Broadway show," he said. On the road, a deep and abiding friendship developed between the tour director and Joshua.

Middlebrooks is fifteen years older, and became the young man's confidant and mentor. It might have been the first time since the age of 14, and all the losses he'd experienced that year, that Joshua again began to trust someone in authority, especially a man. "I was always impressed at Josh's honesty and ownership of his mistakes and his shortcomings, and at his determination to grow beyond them," Middlebrooks said.

Joshua's recollections of his time with the Continentals are filled with joy. Travels with the troupe saw him visit much of the United States and scores of American cities. The tour also brought him to Europe. He traveled to Hamburg, Germany ("really cool, old city"), the Czech Republic ("bought so much crystal, my suitcase weighed a ton"), Switzerland and Denmark. Joshua spent his 17th birthday in Holland staying at a local church member's home. There he ate raw fish on crackers. Before dawn, the children of the household, a brother and sister, excitedly awakened him and brought him to the seaside, where they climbed the highest dyke. "The early morning fog was drifting off the water and flowing like a river down the dyke into the streets and alleys of the brick and thatched roof homes," he would later write of his experience.

Joshua collected postcards from every stop. An avid photographer, he took hundreds and hundreds of pictures of life on the road. He took pictures of performances, of host families, of scenery passing outside the bus window and of tour mates, curled up across a few seats, drooling on their precious pillows. He has photos of Joshua trees, and the cityline sign of Oshkosh, Wisconsin. He took a picture of some of the girls on tour trying to milk a cow ("unsuccessfully I might add," he wrote). In his collection, there are photos of the insides of airports and insides of jet planes. He is particularly proud of a photograph he took of his new best friend. "Mark [was] ready to ring [sic] my neck for hounding him with my camera," Joshua wrote.

While on tour with the Continentals, Joshua hiked the Grand Tetons, snowboarded in the Rockies, ate Swiss chocolate in a café at the base of the Alps. The tour brought him to the top of the St. Louis Arch, the crown of the Statue of Liberty and the rotating lounge in the Seattle Needle. He sat and prayed in a pew of a 600-year-old cathedral in Germany and walked the 400-year-old cobblestone streets in Belgium. "I've stood on the edge of ancient evergreen forest overlooking lush green valleys below," he wrote. In a letter from jail, Joshua described the experience like this:

> *If the old pines could speak they'd recount stories of Teutonic Knights riding out of the mist, full in armor, swords thrust high in iron-covered fists. Thundering hooves shaking the ground, trampling everything in their path . . .*

The Continentals' summer tour was three months long, and for Joshua it went by in an instant. Hugs and tears punctuated the goodbyes, especially in the parting between Joshua and Middlebrooks. But the friends wouldn't be separated for long. Mark had signed up for a Continentals tour that was headed to, among other stops, Trinidad and Tobago. There was an opening in the company for a tech member. Mark gave Joshua a call.

On Joshua's second tour with the Continentals, Mark Middlebrooks didn't serve as tour director. With less responsibility, Mark had more time to get to know his young friend. In Trinidad and Tobago, they were housed together in what Mark describes as a "concrete hut." The structure had no windows, open doorways and was in one of the poorest sections of a very poor city. It was an experience, Middlebrooks says, that makes you "stronger as a person and stronger as friends." From his experience in Trinidad, Joshua came away with a sense of gratitude. "Americans don't realize how good we have it," he once wrote about the trip. "Our worst ghetto is luxury living by comparison."

Nights in the hut and days on streets lined with tarpaper shanties and running with raw sewage, the friendship strengthened. Mark took to calling Joshua his "buddy in the trenches." Joshua had picked up a black-and-red beret somewhere in his travels, and wore it, à la Che Guevara, throughout the trip to Trinidad and Tobago. In an extreme expression of friendship and trust, Joshua one day handed the beret over to his friend. "Never mind, that I no doubt, looked like a complete moron," Mark remembers. "Josh would smile and I would wear it proudly," he said.

When the troupe wasn't performing, Joshua and some of the other Continentals took hikes into the rainforest and spent afternoons on coconut tree–lined beaches with sand, as Joshua describes, "as white as snow made even starker by its proximity to the turquoise waters of the Caribbean." Joshua was quite taken by the beauty of the island, especially the sunsets of the deepest purples and reds. "It stops you in your tracks," he wrote of the experience. There was also occasion for pleasure of the more temporal in Trinidad. One evening the son of a church member turned him on to a local concoction. The coconut milk, lime and sugar mixed with rum and served in a freshly machete-split coconut shell was "Damn good!" Joshua remembers.

But undoubtedly the most searing memory Joshua has of Trinidad is one that perplexes when considered through the events of a rainy July morning many years later in Cheshire.

The troupe's hosts in Trinidad and Tobago were a group of Catholic nuns who "rivaled Mother Teresa," said Mark Middlebrooks. "These women had us running all over the island, singing, sharing, helping, and encouraging," he remembers. Mark was especially moved by how badly AIDS had ravaged the island. According to statistics provided by the United Nations, Tobago suffers one of the highest rates of AIDS deaths in all of the Caribbean. But it was a young girl with a different medical condition who would move Joshua.

Joshua would later describe the building as a "parking garage." The hospital was made of concrete and cinderblock. Joshua had visited it with several of the performing members of the troupe. The tour of the facility brought them into a room that was a makeshift burn unit. Though a hospital official had warned Joshua and the performers, nothing could have prepared them for what they saw. Only 7 or 8, the child, according to Joshua, was horribly disfigured and in terrible pain. He'd heard that her drunken father had thrown the girl into a bonfire. Nothing could be done medically for her. Only death would bring relief. Joshua held her fingertips, the only part that didn't appear burned. In remembering this moment in a letter from jail, he wrote that when he left the hospital he sat in the room used for storage for the troupe's equipment and broke down and cried.

"At the end of our six months together, exhausted and very fulfilled, I said good-bye to Josh," Mark Middlebrooks wrote, remembering their parting. "Other than the leadership team, Josh was the last person from the tour to leave us that day and when he stepped off the bus and headed back into real life, I wept. I truly believe that I saw a young boy grow into a man of great promise through that experience."

In the years that followed, Joshua and Middlebrooks would fall out of touch with one another. The only contact they had was one letter that Joshua sent to Mark a year after the Trinidad and Tobago tour ended telling him that he had joined the Army Reserves. The letter included a photo of Joshua in uniform looking every bit the handsome and confident young man that Middlebrooks had expected him to become. But the picture didn't nearly tell the whole story. Outside influences, inner torment and a seemingly evil inclination had already begun to pull that soldier in the photo down a very dark path. In the following ten years, Joshua would completely turn away from the promise he exhibited on the Continentals tour and the compassion he showed in visiting the young burn victim on the Caribbean island. Instead, Joshua's life would be filled with crime, drugs and jail cells, and it was a path that would eventually lead him to the Petit home on Sorghum Mill Drive.

CHAPTER TWENTY-FOUR

Illuminated by the streetlights, the mist that fell from the night sky gave the block an almost mystical feel. The peaceful silence that engulfed the house at number 300 stood in stark contrast to the quiet horror that was taking place inside. For Dr. Petit, if he was conscious as Joshua claims, the time must have seemed interminable. The almost unbearable pain in his head throbbed with each quickened beat of his heart. The thought of his wife and two daughters held captive, upstairs, and the terrifying, possibilities of what these madmen might do to his family, must have pressured his analytical brain to the point of shutting down.

Joshua lit a Camel, the smell of the acrid smoke so incongruous in the doctor's kitchen. He was thinking about how the plan had changed during the course of the night. Police found crudely made masks, ski hats with eyeholes cut in them. But at some point, Joshua and Hayes abandoned cloaking their identities. Exactly when that happened is not known at this writing. It was a moment, however, that eliminated the chance that this night wouldn't get any worse for the Petits than it had already. Joshua inhaled, then blew the smoke out through his nostrils. You pick your objective, you get in, and then you adjust to the situation, was his method of operation. Perhaps the only constant this night was the reason Joshua picked the Petit house to begin with. Joshua

walked into the bathroom and flushed the cigarette butt.
Then he climbed the stairs to Michaela's bedroom. Tied to
her bed, she looked up at him with eyes that held a fright-
ened incomprehension. Adrenaline mixed with a sexual
urge and raced through Joshua's body like an electric charge.

CHAPTER TWENTY-FIVE

In August of 1996, around the same time Joshua was riding his mountain bike on the Frontier Camp road, Steven Hayes, 33 at the time, was cruising down Hartford's Wethersfield Avenue in a Grand Prix with the windows down and sultry late-summer air blowing across his face. It was nice to be on the outside. As he passed some of the girls, an urge started in his loins and spread throughout his body like a warm virus.

The Grand Prix he was driving was nothing special. A friend owned it. Hayes had inquired about buying the car, and the friend had said maybe, "if you can come up with the cash." That same day, he was on his way to the bank to inquire about a loan. But Wethersfield was lousy with hookers, pushed there by sweeps of Hartford's South End. Twice a day Hayes drove the same route traveling from the community release program on Wyllys Street to his job as a cook at the Chowder Pot out near Hartford-Brainard Airport and back again.

Later, Hayes would tell the cops that he'd stopped the car when he saw a "friend of his," a woman I'll call Tina. He also told police that he hadn't had a drink or drugs in five years. For most of that time Hayes was incarcerated, but the use of drugs and alcohol inside prison walls is commonplace. And records from Northeast Correctional punch holes in Hayes's profession of sobriety. At the end of November of 1993, for instance, he had been given fifteen days in solitary for the possession of "contraband class A," and in March of that year he was also confined to his cell for intoxication. He was disciplined for possessing contraband on two other occasions in Northeast.

But lying and using was a pattern that persisted throughout Hayes's life of incarceration and brief stints of freedom. And so was a pattern of violating parole, which, as Tina leaned into the window of the Grand Prix, he was just about to do again.

Hayes's long-term relationship with Connecticut's Department of Corrections had begun on June 30, 1980, when he was first arrested for third-degree burglary charges, and sentenced to 5 years. He was 17 years old. He had already dropped out of high school. The year before, his father had died. But, according to parole documents, Hayes was having marijuana and alcohol problems for several years before his father's death. Still, during that first incarceration, Hayes gave rehabilitation his most believable attempt . . .

According to parole records, in 1981 he was attending AA meetings in the John R. Manson Youth Institution, part of the Cheshire jail complex. At Manson, Hayes would earn a state high school diploma. In April of 1981, a nun who taught classes at the jail wrote a letter to the parole board on Hayes's behalf. It read in part:

> Steven's been in my class since coming to Cheshire [Manson]. During that time I have observed him growing in seriousness and maturity. He is industrious, ambitious and at all times cooperative and respectful. He has acquired a new interest in the practice of his religion which he seems to be taking seriously.

Although I have been associated in work with inmates for almost ten years and have come to know
hundreds of them, this is the first time I have written a
letter of this kind. I do so because I have faith in Steven's self-rehabilitation. I believe that in returning him
to society at an earlier date, you will be doing something that will prove beneficial to Steven, to society,
and to his own family . . .

By November 1981, he entered his first long-term drug
treatment center, Nascent House, where he stayed for three
months. The project director, Frank Hall, also wrote a letter
to Board of Parole Chairman Richard Reddington, recom-
mending Steven be placed in Project Fire, an addiction services re-entry to society program. In Febuary of 1982, Steven's
mother, Diana, also wrote to Reddington assuring the commissioner that her son had learned his lesson, that she would
open her home to him, and that he would have no problem
finding a job:

Since Steven went to Cheshire last January and then to
Litchfield, I have observed a considerable amount of
maturity in my son. I feel, Steven can be an asset to this
household and in society.
Very truly yours,
Diana J. Hayes

The pleas on Hayes's behalf by the nun and his mother
worked. By February of 1982, Steven was released from
Northeast Correctional Institution and accepted into McCall
House, a halfway house and drug treatment center in Tor-
rington, Connecticut. That April he was released on parole.
And that's when things began to go wrong.

* * *

Hayes's first job during his second chance at a new life was at Curry Auto Body in Torrington, Connecticut. His second chance lasted a total of eight days. Seven of those days he was on a work furlough, still the property of the state of Connecticut. On his first day on parole he would be back in trouble. Though in later incarcerations, Hayes would garner a reputation as a likeable cellmate and prison buddy, he must have made at least one enemy during his stay at his first halfway house. A fellow resident snitched that he'd seen Steven drinking a beer and smoking a joint.

Police arrested Hayes at the auto body shop. Lillian Morton, the woman who ran the halfway house, prepared to expel him from the residence. Hayes vehemently denied the allegations, both to the cops who'd arrested him and to his parole officer. He swore that he'd spent the entire day in question at his mother's. His parole officer wanted to believe him, and begged Ms. Morton to reconsider. The evidence against Hayes was hearsay, he argued.

And it was just hearsay, that is, until Hayes was processed into Litchfield Correctional Center. There, a search of the returning parolee produced a half-ounce of pot.

Back on that August morning on Wethersfield Avenue, Hayes would once again prove his inability to think through his actions. Tina had asked him if he wanted a blast of "ready rock," crack-cocaine. It was only 10 in the morning. But time of day is of little consequence to an addict about to put a torch lighter to the pilot light of his addiction. Already in overdrive with rationalization and lies, Hayes's mind began to plot: The community release program thought he was working. He didn't have to check in until 1:30 a.m. Shit, he thought, he had all the time in the world. Tina hopped into the front seat of the Grand Prix. If things played out the way he hoped, there might be an extra charge for her.

Hayes knew for sure that he was going back to jail. By this time he had plenty of past performance to prove it. But with that realization came a concentrated freedom, the freedom that perhaps only convicts on the run and Zen Buddhists know—the freedom of the moment in which you exist.

The one hit led Steven and Tina to drive to Hartford's North End, a neighborhood then infested with street gangs and crack-cocaine. Hayes bought fifty dollars' worth. He had already cashed his paycheck, and the pay for the seventy hard kitchen hours went in a coke-speeded heartbeat.

Ten o'clock became one o'clock and one o'clock became three just as quick. Time lost its meaning. All he thought about was getting high. All he thought about was sex with Tina. He bought another bag.

At some point, Steven managed to get the Grand Prix back to his friend. By then, he was out of money, and, of course, Tina was long gone. With the August sun now fiery red and low on the horizon, Steven Hayes was a man with few options. To go back to the residence, he knew, was a sure trip back to Northeast Correctional Institution in Mansfield. He'd been out of jail for only three weeks.

Desperate, he hitchhiked up Route 44, making it 16 miles to Canton, where he came upon an abandoned building. It was there where he crashed from the coke high and fell asleep.

At approximately the same time, a staff worker at the community release residence named Walter Decoteau made his rounds. Steven Hayes's bed was empty. But just as Hayes had expected, Decoteau believed that the resident was working. For the prior two weeks Hayes had signed out of the

residence before 10 a.m. and not back in until after 1 a.m.
Two seventy-hour–plus weeks he had worked at the Chowder Pot. It was the dog days of August, not a very busy time
for the restaurant, and undoubtedly the worst time of the
year to work a hot kitchen. But Steven was looking forward
to October 9, when he would be discharged from community release. He had told staff and housemates alike that his
plans included buying his own car and finally providing for
his family. That family included two children and a wife
named Rosalie.[3]

Decoteau at first gave Hayes the benefit of the doubt. Perhaps he had heard Hayes speaking of his future family life.
He'd check the room in an hour, he thought. By then Hayes
would be back. But when the hour passed, and Hayes had
not returned, Decoteau did what he was supposed to do. He
called his supervisor. The supervisor then called the Connecticut State Police. An arrest warrant was prepared. Hayes
became an escaped convict on the run.

Without any money, Hayes's options were limited. He
knew of only two places where he could get cleaned up, have
something to eat, and maybe get some cash. He could either
head west on Route 202 towards Torrington and Rosalie, or
continue northwest on Route 44 to Winsted and his mother's.
He stuck a thumb out as he began to walk backwards down

_____

[3] Not much is known about Rosalie and Hayes's children. Clearly
    though, in one or more periods of freedom, Hayes tried his hand
    at a normal life and fatherhood. But in scores of pages of his pa-
    role records there are only brief mentions of his wife and children.
    In one, when he's petitioning for yet another parole, he writes that
    he is looking forward to getting the chance of making up with his
    son, who is experiencing blackouts that Hayes believes are caused
    by the emotional trauma of his father being in jail.

Route 202. When things seemed hopeless, Hayes always went back to his mother.

Wearing the same clothing he had slept in, his body aching from crack withdrawal, he wasn't exactly a prime candidate for hitchhiking. No cars even slowed down. The August sun beat down on him. But he trudged on. Four miles later he came upon a rest area for the Nepaug Reservoir.

The reservoir was a favored spot for joggers and dog walkers. It was still early, a Saturday morning, and a few cars began to pull into the parking lot. Steven needed to rest. He sat at a picnic table. Just then a brown 1984 Volvo with rust spots entered the parking area. A man got out of the Volvo and began to walk towards the dam access road. As the man disappeared from view, Hayes saw another option.

Hayes went to the car and looked in the windows. The bag, a rainbow-colored straw pocketbook, sat, like an Easter basket, right on the back seat. He looked down around his feet. Some distance away he saw what he needed, a good-sized rock. There was little grace to this burglary. Just the old smash and dash. He reached through the jagged opening in the rear passenger-side window and shook the nuggets of glass from the bag as he pulled it out. There was money in it, twenties, tens. About $60 altogether. His heart quickened. He swiveled his head back and forth, but saw nothing, no movement. No one had heard. As he rooted through the bag, he found a set of car keys.

Two minutes later, he was headed down Route 202, his fortunes dramatically changed for the better. Perhaps the thought came to him to just keep driving. Head west until he came upon the Pacific Ocean. There would be plenty of unattended cars to break into along the way. But it was a thought that lasted just about the time it took him to think of another hit of ready rock, and another hooker. The desire was overwhelming. He turned the Volvo and headed back to Hartford.

The day that followed went pretty much as had the day before. It takes forty-eight hours for crack-cocaine to clear from the system. As illegal drugs go, the detox from crack is quick. But during that first forty-eight hours the physical urge to get high is immense. Then the psychological urge kicks in and lasts much longer. Under the lash of both of these physical and mental masters, the addict has only one charge: to find and use the drugs.

In the world of crack addiction, $60 buys a high that goes up in smoke in a matter of minutes. But somehow, Steven managed to fund a full day of smoking rock and paying for hookers. When he was finally spent, he ended up sleeping in the same abandoned building as he had the night before.

The next day, day three of his escape, he awoke with a mission. He drove back to the reservoir parking lot and cruised for opportunity. This time, though, he used a hammer he'd found in the Volvo instead of a rock.

As criminal minds go, Steven's was far from that of an evil genius. Back in 1986, when he was stopped by cops for driving a brown Chevy station wagon with an expired emissions sticker and Massachusetts plates that belonged to an '80 Subaru, a search of the car revealed a white container that held a "brown, leafy substance," according to the police report. Hayes told the cops it was herbs that he used as a cook at a local restaurant. A field test proved the substance to be marijuana, and Steven was arrested.

As Hayes's crack run continued, time leaped, crawled and then flattened into a gray expanse without definition. Later, he would say that he thought his escape had lasted about six or seven days, a week of crack highs and crime that included breaking into seven cars, using a stolen Fleet Bank check-book to forge two checks that he made out to himself and trying to use a stolen credit card to buy a radio in a department store in Camden. The card was denied.

His estimate was short by four days and several crimes. On September 10, eleven days after his spree had begun, he again pulled into the reservoir parking lot, still driving the brown Volvo. The rear window was still missing.

He turned the engine off and sat in the quiet car. "I wish the whole thing was over," he said—or, better yet, had never happened. It was then that he saw the state trooper cruiser slowly pull in front of him. For a moment, he sat there motionless, his eyes trained on the trooper, feeling like a frightened animal. He was just about to give up. Then he slammed the gearshift into drive.

Later Steven would admit to "going very fast," but the chase, like most of the previous week-and-a-half, seemed like an out-of-body experience. He remembered hearing the Trooper's siren and then seeing the flashing lights. And he remembered that he'd taken a turn too fast and driven off the road. It was Country Club Road in Avon, Connecticut, according to the police report.

Then Steven lay on the side of the road, his face pressed against the ground, his hands cuffed behind his back. It was finally over. His jail sentence was 5 years for third-degree larceny. Hayes was about to go back to the only place where he really knew how to exist.

By then, Hayes had spent the majority of his adult life behind bars. Most of his criminal activity came in a desultory attempt to support his drug addiction. He had been convicted of burglary, firearms possession, drug possession, forgery, larceny and escape. He had spent jail time in Hartford Correctional Center, Cheshire Correctional Institution, Litchfield Correctional Center, Osborn Correctional Institution, Bridgeport Correctional Center, Bergin Correctional Institution, Corrigan-Radgowski Correctional Center, MacDougall–Walker Correctional Institution, Robinson Correctional Institution, Willard–Cybulski Correctional Institution, Enfield Correctional Institution, John R. Manson Youth Institution, Brooklyn Correctional Institution and Gates Correctional Institution. While in jail, he had racked up over twenty disciplinary tickets, mostly for intoxication and having contraband (i.e., drugs or alcohol). He was also disciplined for fighting. On numerous occasions, Steven was denied parole. In 1995, a letter from Linda Thomas, a paroles hearing officer, listed four reasons why Steven's parole was denied:

1. The extensive criminal history that you have generated.
2. Your poor institutional adjustment as evidenced by the number and type of disciplinary reports you have accumulated.
3. The repetitive nature of your convictions.
4. Your poor performance while on previous periods of community release and probation.

He had failed the state in numerous attempts at rehabilitation. Hayes had been in no fewer than seven halfway houses/community release programs. He'd completed only three of them. In the other four he'd either tried to escape, was found to have pending charges or violated the rules.

While in jail in the fall of 2000, Steven wrote a letter to the parole board:

*I am scared to go back out unsupervised. Everyday
I feel myself slipping back to where I want never to
return . . . I am afraid of a future without recovery.*

Fellow inmates, he wrote, were advising him to serve his time
and be discharged. That way, the jailhouse chorus reasoned,
no one could tell him what to do. "I NEED SOMEONE TO
TELL ME WHAT TO DO," Steven wrote in block letters.

That fall, Hayes had been sent back to jail from Warner
House, a small treatment facility in central Connecticut. He
had been caught with a cell phone, a violation of the halfway
house's rules. He told the staff of Warner House that the
phone belonged to his sister-in-law, that he was only borrow-
ing it. But an investigation proved that he had rented the
phone himself, in his sister-in-law's name. He'd had the phone
for almost a month before they caught him.

Hayes tried to weasel his way out of his predicament in a
letter to the parole board:

*. . . addiction is serious, and for me it is deadly seri-
ous. To an addict the phone is one of the most important tools to recovery. When an addict feels the need
to get high he uses the phone to call his sponsor or
another addict in the N.A. Program. During my stay
at the Warner house that phone stopped me from getting high 2–6 times a day. I do understand that I broke
a rule having that phone. If I had known it would return me to jail I would have made a different choice.
But to be honest my only thought was to my recovery
program. Staying clean was my first concern.*

But when he was searched, Hayes had $360 in cash on him,
suspicious at best, and in violation of the rules of the half-

way house, which permitted residents a $35 a week limit. Steven represented himself at the parole hearing. He was unsuccessful, and was remanded to Osborn Correctional Institution on 11/14/00. On January 4, 2001, his parole was officially rescinded by letter. He took the news by getting high in jail, and blamed his situation on the collapse of his support system. Still petitioning the parole board, Steven wrote:

> *With nobody to talk to and share my feelings and problems with, in January I relapsed. When I was returned for having the phone everything began to fall apart on me. I was taken away from things I began to rely on and thrust back into a negitive enviorment.[4]*

When Steven's urine sample in jail came up dirty, he was disciplined for intoxication and given 8 days of punitive segregation, 30 days without recreation and 30 days without social visitors.

> *Worse yet, I blew 23 months of clean time. As soon as I got high I let myself down along with everybody who cares for me. My sponsor always said relaps is part of recovery because it means something is missing in my life. What is missing is my support system.*

This time, Steven's pleas to the parole board went unrequited. He served his time.

Records show that Steven's life behind bars now was relatively docile. He was, for all intents and purposes,

------

[4] Throughout the book, in written quotes from both Hayes and Joshua, spelling has not been corrected.

institutionalized. In earlier incarcerations he had been disciplined for fighting and other violent actions. As his years in jail went by, violence became less of an option. Longtime convicts learn to swim silently through the dangerous waters in jail. But that's not to say that Hayes wasn't capable of violence on the outside. Parole records show three arrests for weapons charges. A search after he was arrested for stealing a '75 Chevy revealed an ice pick on him.

Some of Hayes's reluctance to engage other inmates had to do with his rather unimposing stature. Unlike some jail-buffed con, Stephen had become pudgy behind bars, and he'd developed male-pattern baldness. As his years in jail accumulated, Steven was more a target than an aggressor.

In 1996, Hayes was transferred between correctional facilities by the Hartford County Sheriff's Department. A remark was made in the back of the transport van that led to an altercation. Steven was beaten quite seriously. "No matter how loud I yelled for the sheriffs' attention, I received no help," Hayes wrote in his civil complaint. "Because of the way these trucks are set up and the amount of inmates that are put in the rear of these trucks, there is no way to supervise the actions within." Steven suffered a ruptured tendon in his wrist during the attack.

But both Hayes's docile nature in his later years in jail, and his clown-like facade covered an anger that simmered within. It came, this discontent, from years of bad breaks, years of incarceration, years of disappointing everyone in his life. Even his mother, Diana, who supported her son, both financially and emotionally, and wrote letter after letter on his behalf, had begun to lose faith. A Hayes family member once said, "There is no good side [to Steven]."

Hayes might have kept his anger stuffed down, but to believe that he was no longer capable of violence denies a basic nature of the kind of criminal he was. Like an old, caged dog, Hayes looked harmless behind bars. But on the outside he was quite a different animal.

In October of 2001, after he had served his full sentence for his eleven-day burglary and crack-cocaine run, Hayes began one of the longest periods of freedom in his adult life—about eighteen months. He was working, according to his parole records, in a bakery called the Big Y in Torrington. He insisted that he was faithfully attending Alcoholics Anonymous and Narcotics Anonymous meetings. He had dozens of NA meetings to choose from in the area where he worked and lived, including one in Torrington that was held three times a week.

He also professed a concern for his family during this time. Some months before his release, Steven wrote a letter to his parole officer. In it, he mentioned two "personal problems." One was the cancer that his grandmother had developed. At the time, his grandmother was 90. The other problem was about his son's blackouts due to stress. "That stress is because I came into his life after being away for 7 years and then disappeared again," Steven wrote. "I don't want to continue to hurt people I care about . . ."

Hayes was constitutionally incapable of being honest, a key ingredient to staying sober. Without sobriety, his words were the empty exaltations of an addict. In February 2002, after Steven had gunned his mother's 1990 Grand Am past a slower vehicle in a no-passing lane, he was pulled over by a state trooper. Hayes consented to a search of his person and vehicle. The officer found a bag of marijuana and a pipe stuffed down between the seat and console. Steven told the trooper that he was trying to live a "clean lifestyle," and that a friend had given him the pot.

Like his sobriety, Steven's freedom was always short-lived. The countdown for his return to jail would start the moment he walked out the prison door. And if there was any doubt that he had a limited criminal mind, that thought is put to rest by his actions in the fall of 2003.

It's doubtful that Steven stealing the Volvo seven years before was the only reason that prompted the Connecticut state cops to keep the Nepaug Reservoir parking lot under surveillance. Other thieves must have preyed on the joggers' and nature walkers' cars. The cops were posted in lookout positions. On foot, one cop was 25 yards deep into the woods that surround the reservoir parking lot. The other officer was watching the entrance.

Simple deduction dictates that Hayes's pot smoking had again escalated into something more. And again Hayes need cash to keep the high going. The cop in the woods noticed the gray Ford Escort enter the parking lot, and the heavy, balding man get out and open the hood. Several other cars pulled into and out of the parking lot. Steven then slammed closed the hood and stood looking around for a couple of minutes. He then got back into the Escort and left.

A half hour later, he returned. By this time, the Escort had garnered the full attention of the cops. Steven sat in the Escort watching the trickle of cars pulling in and out of the lot. After approximately ten minutes, he got out the car and walked down the service road that led to Nepaug Dam, looking for anyone on their way back to the lot. Convinced that the coast was clear, he ran back and began peering in the windows of the parked cars.

In the woods, not more than 25 feet from Hayes, the cop watched the whole show. When Steven found what he was looking for, he walked quickly over to the Escort, pulled something out from under the front seat, and returned to the minivan bearing the Connecticut plates. The driver of the van had left the purse on the front seat. Steven took the rock he held in his hand and smashed the passenger-side window. As he did, the cop bolted from the woods, his gun drawn.

"Police! Stop! Get on the ground and show me your hands!"

Steven ran. He ran as fast and far as he could down the path, but his dash was neither quick nor lengthy. Soon he was out of breath. He dropped the purse and put his hands in the air. "I'm about to shit my pants," he said to the cop. "I'm not going anywhere."

But he was.

The mug shot taken two days later shows a fat-faced Steven with thin lips. His jaw is clenched, the corners of his mouth are turned down and his eyes are expressionless. The date of the photograph was October 1, 2003. He was given 5 years for the burglary, a sentence that, if served in full, would have kept him in jail until May of 2008, which, of course, would have made it impossible for him to be on Sorghum Mill Drive on July 23, 2007. But the Connecticut Department of Correction gambled that it was not very likely for Hayes to act in a violent manner, or be at all detrimental to society.

They couldn't have been more wrong.

CHAPTER TWENTY-SIX

Outside, the rain fell harder now. It thumped rhythmically off the trampoline in the driveway. Upstairs in the Petit house, quiet sounds of disbelief and fear seeped from behind the closed doors of the bedrooms. The Petit girls, their hands and feet zip-tied, were bound to their beds. As the night crept by, Joshua walked from bedroom to bedroom checking on his hostages, while Hayes rooted through drawers and closets. He had looted Mrs. Petit's jewelry, which included a string of pearls. He grabbed a jar of coins that Michaela had collected for M.S.; he stuffed what he could in a sack: a couple of cell phones, including one encrusted with fake jewels, maybe a couple of hundred in cash from pocketbooks and the doctor's wallet. It was far from the score that Hayes had envisioned and hoped for. It was far from the money he needed get his own place.

But it's ludicrous to believe that Steven Hayes's plan was still to score enough money for an apartment deposit. Conditions of his parole dictated he couldn't leave Connecticut, and how could he live anywhere within a thousand miles of the Petit house after the crimes he'd already committed this night—after a home invasion, armed with zip ties to take hostages? Even given his prior criminal ineptness, he couldn't have been that dumb.

But Hayes's shortcoming as a criminal didn't mean he

lacked imagination in other areas. "He was a little per-
verted," said a halfway-house pal of Hayes's. Months after
the murders, in a jailhouse interview, Joshua said that
Hayes had a curious reading list of books he'd checked out
of a prison library. The books dealt with rape and bondage.
Hayes wanted something out of this night, this risk. And if it
wasn't going to be enough money, perhaps it was going to
be something else.

CHAPTER TWENTY-SEVEN

By the time he was 18, Joshua had already forged quite a life story. He had spent his formative years on an expansive, wooded estate. Home schooled, and surrounded with formidable educational influences, he had accumulated a core curriculum few of his peers could match. He was also a juvenile delinquent with a rap sheet that included home burglary and arson. And he had already had a moment of redemption. But he was only 18, and there were chapters of his life yet to be written.

Whatever positive emotional effect the Continentals tour had on Joshua didn't last long. Back home in Cheshire, he found himself in trouble and, by the time he was 18, back in front of a judge. Once again the judge would decide against sending Joshua to jail. And though, at first, it seemed as if the judge's decision might set Joshua on the right path, it would soon become a road that would take him far away from his Christian life, and closer to a rainy morning on Sorghum Mill Drive. According to Joshua, this part of his story begins like this:

Joshua and his best friend had traveled to a nearby town to go shopping in a Bob's sporting goods store. There, the friend saw a pair of sneakers that he really liked. He had one small problem: He didn't have the money to pay for them.

Now Joshua qualifies this story by making it clear that what the friend was about to attempt was an aberration. For most of Joshua's life, this friend had been the voice of reason. By all accounts, he was a law-abiding, productive and likable kid. Perhaps the sneakers were just too tempting, or, more likely, Joshua's own criminal aura had rubbed off on him. Whatever the motivation, the friend came up with an idea.

If there is any lingering belief that the friend had a calculating criminal mind, it dissolves with the description of his plan, which mostly involved trying on the new pair of sneakers and then walking out the door with them.

"Brilliant!" Joshua says with a smile in remembering the heist.

It's no surprise that the two friends didn't get far from the store before a beefy security guard tackled them. The police were called, and both were frisked.

It is at this moment when the hot searchlight of the law sweeps from the friend to Joshua. In one of Joshua's pockets was a knife with a double-edged blade. He was arrested for carrying a concealed weapon.

Given Joshua's prior record, and the court-ordered stipulations attached to his freedom, his arrest could have led to jail time. His parents hired a lawyer.

At the time, Joshua had given joining the U.S. Army some consideration. He was a buff, to say the least. Along with a childhood filled with playing soldier on his grandfather's estate, he says he owns every John Wayne movie ever made, and most of the war films of Audie Murphy. Joshua happened to mention his intention to his lawyer.

"Perfect," the counselor answered. "I'll tell the judge."

The judge, a no-nonsense fellow who had in front of him Joshua's sheet, which then included the Huxley garage fire and the burglaries, called the young defendant to the bench.

"You have a week to get your sorry ass into basic training or I'll throw it in jail," he said peering over his eyeglasses. Two days later Joshua was in a recruiter's office, and soon after that, was on his way as a U.S. Army Reservist to the Ozarks and Fort Leonard Wood, or, as Joshua likes to call it, "Fort Lost in the Woods."

If something outside of him could fix Joshua, the Army seemed like the place where that could happen. And, at first, Joshua looked like a fit for the Army. Years later, in a letter from jail, Joshua wrote that he thought he would have made a fine soldier, "had I not been so young (18) and given to distraction."

He did complete both basic and advanced training. In advanced, he became Army-certified in both heavy equipment and explosives. "They were paying me to blow shit up," he would later say with glee.

He was an enthusiastic soldier, and garnered the respect of his superiors. "My officers loved me," he wrote.

His goal was to become a sniper. And, according to Army records, Joshua received a Sharpshooter Marksmanship Qualification Badge with a Grenade Bar and a Marksman Marksmanship Qualification Badge with a Rifle Bar. There is little doubt that Joshua would have been a crackerjack sniper. The love of guns ran in Joshua's family, especially with his Aunt Tanya.

Tanya is Ben and Christopher Komisarjevsky's older sister. In 1959, Tanya married George Metaksa, a mechanical engineer. Metaksa was a skeet and competitive pistol shooter, an avocation that rubbed off on his new wife. The couple joined pistol shooting clubs. In 1981, Tanya began working for the United States Senator from New York, Alphonse D'Amato, as his legislative director. In 1991, she was elected to the National Rifle Association's board of directors, and rose to become the NRA's chief lobbyist, a position that the magazine *Mother Jones* said made her one of the most powerful women in Washington. "Everyone in my family is a member of the NRA," Joshua would boast in remembering his aunt.[5]

Undoubtedly, Joshua had the inclination and aptitude to be a good soldier. Ten years after his training, Joshua could, almost to the letter, recite the 1998 basic training small arms field manual. But Joshua and his family had done little to address his emotional problems. And even though he could keep his demons at bay for stretches, it was only a matter of time before they'd claw their way to the surface.

Joshua's Army career would go no further than advanced training.

In response to a Freedom of Information Act request, the U.S. Army released only eleven pages of sixty-five documents that comprised Joshua's Army file. The Army contends that release of the withheld pages would "clearly result in an unwarranted invasion of personal privacy." The Army also refused to share any recorded internal advice, recommendations or "subjective evaluations pertaining to the decision-making process of an agency." Joshua himself seemed embarrassed when he talked or wrote about the events that had led to his discharge. A little background, however, might offer an explanation.

---

[5] In 1997, Tanya authored a book called *Safe Not Sorry: Keeping Yourself and Your Family Safe in a Violent Age*. The book has been described as a guide for personal safety for women. Given what would happen in Cheshire in July of 2007, the irony of Aunt Tanya's title speaks for itself.

The Komisarjevskys had a modest summer cabin in Alton Bay, New Hampshire. As picturesque a setting as you can find, Alton Bay is part of Lake Winnipesaukee, a giant body of water that covers some 72 square miles and has 365 islands—"one for every day," is the locals' expression. The granite foothills of the White Mountains surround the lake which was once used as the backdrop for the Bill Murray movie *What About Bob?* It is also not far from another lake made famous in the movie *On Golden Pond.*

The area has a strong Christian community, which, along with its natural beauty, attracted the Komisarjevskys. It was in Alton Bay where Joshua began to date his second significant girlfriend. Rebecca (her name changed here) was the daughter of yet another youth pastor in Joshua's life. According to Joshua, Rebecca was attracted to the "bad boy" streak in him, which seemed to widen in her presence. One winter night, in the process of showing off, Joshua almost blew off his own head.

He had gotten his hands on a canister of gunpowder and came up with the bright idea to write Rebecca's name in script with the powder and light it ablaze. He says he thought the powder was fireworks grade, but that it actually turned out to be musket powder. The blast nearly lifted him off the ground. Joshua reacted by blindly shoving his face into a snow bank, one that was filled with road salt and sand.

During the night in the hospital—the first of an extended stay—Rebecca held Joshua's hand as he slipped in and out of consciousness. For years afterwards, he said, he experienced flashbacks of the explosion, where he would imagine his skin melting off his face. But in the immediate aftermath, it was Rebecca who nursed Joshua back to health.

In looking back on his relationship with Rebecca, Joshua

uses the word "co-dependent" to describe its primary flaw. It is known that Joshua began going to Cocaine Anonymous meetings early in his teens. His exposure to the 12-step culture and its excavation of family of origin problems indicates that he was at least involved in some form of group therapy, even if it was just C.A. meetings. It also indicates that Joshua had, early in his life, added addiction to his emotional struggles. According to Joshua, Rebecca shared those same problems.

Joshua's troublesome persona fed into Rebecca's co-dependency. She wanted to save him almost as much as she wanted to be with him. This reliance was a breeding ground for maladaptive and compulsive behavior, on both their parts.

They also shared a propensity for slipping into deep depression. It was during these dark times when the worst of their behavior began to show. Joshua called the relationship a "fatalistic attraction," with emotions that ran very hot.

It was a time in both their lives when they struggled with identity issues and adolescent sexual passions. Because of the intense religious surroundings, the "all-seeing eye of the church," as Joshua called it, they also felt a great deal of conflict and guilt. None of these feelings are unusual in the least. But it was how Rebecca and Joshua found relief from the emotional discomfort that is alarming.

As Joshua described it; Sinners, guilty of our mutually burning desires "possessed" with the "evil" spirits . . . we privately cut our own skin releasing the meloncoly deep within through the letting of our own blood.

Among young people, self-mutilation is an alarmingly popular phenomenon. Experts believe that the behavior is spread from one person to another just like a communicable disease.

Although it's not known when Rebecca started, we do know that Joshua had been cutting himself long before he met her. Along with the word "HATE" that he'd carved into his arm after the police had come to his house, the scars on Joshua's arms tell a story of a long-term battle with this affliction. There is a school of psychological thought that believes cutting is a form of suicide prevention. The cutter, usually a child between the ages of 5–15, mostly girls but not always, self-mutilate to manage the constant refrain in their thoughts that tells them they would be better off dead. It throws the suicidal tendency a bone, if you will.

Many times, cutting is set off by a childhood psychological trauma, such as spousal abuse and, of course, sexual abuse. Joshua had never let the emotional wounds he'd suffered in his childhood bedroom heal enough to scar. "I lost sight of purpose, I forgot to live," he would later say of this time of his life. In a letter from jail, he wrote about the lasting effects of the sexual abuse:

> My trouble buried so deeply inside nothing less than a miracle could set me free. Living trapped within the confines of social restraint, trapped within even my own skin, I've been alone, drifting in the empty darkness unreachable, burdened with a terrible knowledge I couldn't share and which no one else could understand.
>
> All I wanted was to disappear from house and home and spare all, this cancer in me to disappear into the darkness outside and roam in the night until I finally found release from the pain within my mind and my spirit calmed once more.

According to Joshua, Rebecca was devastated when he joined the Reserves. "She had a hard time staying away from me for a day, never mind for the time I was in basic and advanced," he says.

After advanced training, Joshua either went to New Hampshire on leave, or was sent to a U.S. Army Reserve training center in Rochester, New Hampshire—it's not clear from the records which. In either case, he was back near Rebecca, who was still deeply depressed over his departure. "She was a wreck," Joshua remembered of the girl to whom he returned. He was worried what she would do if he left her again. So worried, that staying with Rebecca took precedence over his commitment to the Army. He would not return to the Reserves.

But it's hard to believe that taking care of his co-dependent girlfriend was the only reason Joshua walked away from the Reserves and it wasn't.

Although he didn't really have much of a choice in joining he Army, Joshua was proud of the fact that he'd completed his training. But when he returned home on leave, he thought that people in his church and other friends had turned their backs on him. As he recounted:

> *I had come home from basic training in the Army thinking they would be proud of me, when in reality I was slapped across the face by the ones most dear to me.*

Joshua was vague on just who was doing the slapping. Undoubtedly, there was some lingering animosity towards him among those who had put their faith in him.

He had already accumulated a track record for disappointing youth pastors and other church officials. "I became their whipping boy," Joshua wrote of his relationship with church members at this time, "a scapegoat for anything that went wrong." Parents and pastors of the church thought Joshua was a corruptive influence to the other youths, who, according to

Joshua, "had similar sins to him." At least one New Hampshire church group banished Joshua and his entire family. The letter read in part: "You are not welcome to return."

Rebecca's father has a vivid picture in his mind's eye of Joshua from the days just before he joined the Army. In this mental snapshot, he sees Joshua with multi-colored hair, baggy pants and a wallet held to a wide black belt with a chain—the picture more of a troubled kid than one looking for trouble.

But, here again, it's hard to believe that Joshua went AWOL because he didn't get the recognition he thought he deserved from friends and church members—that is, unless a third ingredient is added.

In describing his drug use at this time, Joshua has two different memories. On one hand, he talks as if he lived a happy-go-lucky, flower child–like existence. "I became a self made connoisseur of sorts in matters regarding marijuana," he wrote of this time in his life. "Everyday was like a walk through a park in Amsterdam."

Though Joshua waxes romantic about this time of his life, the truth of the matter was he was on the run, and, as will later emerge, he was using illegal drugs far more dangerous than marijuana.

Though he wrote that the break-up was "long and messy," the relationship with Rebecca seemed to fade rather quickly from Joshua's life. With the Army wondering about the whereabouts of their reservist, Joshua was sneaking into an Alton Bay church dormitory to sleep. Though the events are cloudy, it seems as though Rebecca was the one who told church elders about Joshua's sleeping arrangements. It was at that point that Joshua put Rebecca behind him.

In the beginning of August of 1998, just a few days before his 19th birthday, and a little less than ten months after he'd joined the Army Reserve, Joshua made his way to North Conway, a resort town in New Hampshire. There he got a job at a ski resort called Mount Cranmore.

The work at the resort was hard, clearing trails with chainsaws and bladed Weedwhackers. But the money was ok, the White Mountains were beautiful and the Army and Rebecca seemed a lifetime away.

One day during a break, a co-worker, a guy who hadn't said a word to Joshua up until that point, asked for a light for a joint he held between his lips. Joshua struck up a match and a friendship in that same moment. Brian and Joshua eventually rented a house together in North Conway. The two friends stayed in the tourist town for several seasons.

There were parties at the home they shared just about every night. Though now only 19, Joshua still had his Army I.D., and began to frequent the local and tourist bars at night. "After a few days, I was a regular and not carded," he wrote. Both Brian and Joshua also worked for a company that cleaned swimming pools. Often those who attended their house parties would end the night skinny-dipping in a stranger's swimming pool to which Joshua had the keys.

The house they shared became known as "party central," and Joshua flourished as a sort of an entertainment director. "Anything was better than boredom of the self-reflection that comes in the stillness of tranquility," he would later write of his hard-partying ways.

Home from work, tired and dirty, Joshua would smoke a joint. Brian seemed content to watch a movie or just hang out. But Joshua would take a shower and a need for excitement would slowly build. Lying on the couch, Brian would smile and shake his head as he watched his roommate get ready for his trips into town.

In the basement of the house was a glass-topped coffee

table. Joshua had begun to dabble in dealing drugs, mostly to partiers who came back to the house. The table in the basement served as his cutting board. With a blast of cocaine up his nose, and enough in a package to fuel a couple of new friends for the evening, Joshua would jump on his mountain bike and head into town.

His taste was eclectic when it came to nightlife. Sometimes he would head to touristy bars and sometimes to the hard-partying townie joints. In any venue, he had the same M.O.: he would search for "pretty faces" and ask them back to the house for after-hours parties. He was quite successful.

Joshua had a way with women. It didn't matter if they were older, younger or his own age, they all seemed to fall under his spell. Articulate even in his teens, gracious and polite, Joshua was a disarming conversationalist. "My warring characteristics have, among other things, translated into a 'mysteriously' charismatic appeal that has drawn people to me over the years," Joshua explains. "I've been told that I could charm a serpent and [be] just as cold as a snake, not exactly the most flattering of compliments but I'll take it. I've been called worse."

With his innocent skateboarder looks and pocket filled with amphetamines, he was a lethal combination. As Joshua would write in a letter from jail:

> I brought smiles and good cheer wherever I went. No money for a few drinks? I got ya, it's on me . . . No bud to smoke and lifes beating you down? I got ya, let's roll one up . . . Down on your luck and strung out jonesing for one more hit? I got ya.

But Joshua's life at this point was far from all fun and games. And the escalation of his drug use was alarming. By his own admission, he had by this time begun smoking crystal-meth and mainlining cocaine. And his core emotional problems still remained unattended.

When the party died out, and the drugs and money were all spent, Joshua was left alone with himself—and, by his own admission, he wasn't very good company. Joshua says that he would, coming off of a drug binge, sit in a room with a bottle of Southern Comfort and a .38-caliber revolver with a single bullet in the chamber and play Russian roulette.

It was as though his head had split apart anyhow. He hated himself without relief. He hated the namby-pamby kid who had been forced into sexual acts with a boy. He hated the Christian phony he could be. He hated coming off drugs. He hated that he'd failed in the Army. He hated that he always failed, "one step forward, two steps back," he'd say.

In hundreds of pages of letters written in jail, his stories chart his emotional swings. Some of them, like his description of Russian roulette, come from a desperate place, and others are filled with manic bravado. And throughout, his ever-escalating drug use amplified his cyclic episodes.

As he'd swing back up on this never-ending bipolar amusement ride, he'd fancy himself the tough guy and try to live up to a criminal facade. *Look at how tough I am!* his actions would shout. But more a troubled child than a criminal, he wasn't really tough at all. And in the empty silence of a room, with a gun to his temple, he'd want to silence the voices that screamed within. Each spin of the revolver's cylinder was a 1-in-6 chance of ending his misery. He would later write about this time in his life, saying:

> *The ones closest to me saw me as hopeless, and I was bound and determined to show them just how hopeless one could become.*

Joshua's stay in North Conway was short, but not without lasting implications. As many of his relationships seemed to do, his friendship with Brian flared hot and then burned out quickly. Surreptitiously, or as far under the radar as he could manage, Joshua moved back to Cheshire, but did so with several criminal contacts.

It was in North Conway, Joshua says, where he was introduced to marijuana suppliers who moved tons of pot from the Canadian border down the Eastern Seaboard. Though in one sense the move back to Cheshire was a kid running home to Mommy and Daddy, it was also a move up the criminal ladder.

CHAPTER TWENTY-EIGHT

Joshua's desertion from the Army didn't exactly initiate a full-scale manhunt. In fact, during the late 1990s, and facing a manpower shortage, the Army was reluctant to prosecute AWOL cases. In 1994, there were some 1,500 Army deserters, a number that rose steadily to over 4,000 by the end of the decade. Only 6 percent of those cases ended in military court-martials. The other 94 percent concluded in discharges rated less than honorable. Although the phrase "Army deserter" conjures the Vietnam War and conscientious objectors heading to Canada, very few AWOL cases are political in motivation. According to Kathy Dolby, who wrote extensively for *Harper*'s magazine on the subject, most AWOL cases "quietly return home and hope nobody notices."

Joshua's return to Cheshire might have been predictable, though his behavior once he arrived, however, was anything but.

Joshua pulled his Chevy Silverado onto an exit ramp off the highway just north of Springfield, Massachusetts. His "associate," as he called the fellow riding shotgun, needed a bathroom break.

The run had begun at the Canadian/Vermont border and was headed straight down Route 91 to the heart of Connecticut.

Joshua was a cautious deliveryman. And the least of his worries was the cops, he would say. According to Joshua, it was 4-to-1 odds that if something went wrong, it would be due to a rival dealer or a gang-banger, rather than law enforcement.

He picked this particular exit because it led to a small town, and it would be easier to spot any vehicle that might pose a problem. The gas station he pulled into was straight out of a Norman Rockwell painting, with "antique-looking fuel pumps out front." But the glass-fronted, small brick building also had the usual modern advertisements for cigarettes, lottery tickets and weekly specials written in black felt marker on fluorescent whiteboard. A warm Indian summer afternoon, there was just a hint of a chill in the breeze. "It was one of those perfect New England days," Joshua wrote.

As his associate dashed to the bathroom on the side of the building, Joshua sat behind the wheel of the Silverado, leaning against the door. The big engine purred in idle.

Just then, "a 1960s version of Noah's Ark," as Joshua describes it, pulled into the parking lot next to an air pump. From the boat with wheels stepped a little old lady, "easily in her 80s," according to Joshua. For a few minutes he watched as the woman tried to wrestle the snake of an air hose. And, for a moment, he was torn between staying put in the truck and safeguarding his haul, or giving the elderly gal a hand. Between the seat and the center console was a holster that Joshua had devised and installed. In the holster was a 9mm Beretta. It was one of two identical handguns Joshua owned. He called them "his twins." He took the Beretta and slid it into his pants at the small of his back, put on his leather sports coat and stepped out of the truck.

The lady was trying to unravel the hose as Joshua approached her from behind. When he was just a step or two from her, he rattled the truck keys in his left hand and she turned her head, startled. Joshua grinned.

"May I be of assistance?" Joshua said, turning on the charm.

"Why, yes," the woman replied brightly.

Joshua filled all four tires, and was about to hang the hose back up when the little old lady asked if he would mind blowing out the air filter. "My late husband would always do that," she added with a wisp of sadness in her voice.

Joshua complied, all the while smiling. When he'd finished, he asked if there was anything else she needed. The lady shook her head no, then touched his cheek with the tips of her fingers and told him what a nice boy he was.

In the meantime, his associate had made his way back to the Silverado. He was shaking his head as Joshua finally walked back to the truck. They had forty-six pounds of high-grade marijuana, called "Northern Lights," in the back, worth more than $70,000 to the dealer. And here was Joshua doing his Christian Brigade act with some crusty old gal. "You didn't check the fluids," his partner said with a smirk.

"Don't be a wiseass," Joshua replied, as he pulled the Beretta out and slid it back in the holster. He then turned the key and the Silverado growled to life.

"Ah, fifty-two to base, be advised," said the associate in his best police dispatcher's voice. "Armed and dangerous subjects have made a pit-stop and are now assisting little old lady with routine vehicle maintenance, how should we proceed? Over." Joshua laughed and gunned the Silverado back towards the highway and Hartford.

It must have been all those black-and-white movies Joshua

saw as a child that prompts him to recall his time transporting illegal drugs as though Frank Capra had scripted it. But if Joshua is to be taken at his word—and considering his current legal situation, there is little reason not to—he had gone from selling small amounts of cocaine to his partying friends in North Conway, to becoming a major marijuana mule in less than a year.

He was far from Jimmy Stewart. The price for the marijuana had already been negotiated—$1,700 a pound—and with forty-six pounds in his truck, it was Joshua's job to deliver the pot to Connecticut, collect nearly $80,000, and bring the cash back to the supplier in Vermont. Joshua's take was 15 percent plus a pound of product, free and clear, that, most of the time, he'd smoke himself and give away to friends. After he paid his associate and other expenses, Joshua says that he made nearly $6,000 for the day's work, of approximately a 400-mile round trip.

According to the U.S. Department of Justice, Joshua's route was part of the "New England pipeline" of drug transportation, connecting the two major consumers on the East Coast, Boston and New York City, and as a conduit through which illegal drugs flow from Canada. A D.O.J. website from 2002 describes Interstate 91 as a main drug courier route, and Interstate 84 as an extension to southwestern Connecticut and the cities of Danbury, Waterbury, and Hartford to New York and Pennsylvania.

By the late 1990s, Joshua wrote, he was transporting marijuana in quantities upwards of fifty pounds at a time:

> It was my supplier, my truck, my risk therefore putting me in a strong position to negotiate favorable terms depending on who I was dealing with and how much I did or didn't like them.

According to Joshua, the original buyer/dealer could make up to 120 percent on their investment, depending on the scope of their network and what degree of control they possessed on their submarket.

There are huge variances in profit margin related to how much direct involvement the supplier had and the level of managerial skill they possessed. "If they wanted to nickel-and-dime every gram, they'd make huge profits, but they'd have to personally interact with hundreds of people, making their risk of getting caught that much greater, as well as prolonging the time between reorders, thus weakening their trading position," he stated.

If, on the other hand, the supplies sold at wholesale, they'd make a lower return on investment, but would only be known to a smaller-knit group of people, limiting their exposure to law enforcement and other criminals.

"These are the dealers I enjoyed doing business with, because they make their profit by volume, which meant more reorders and translated into more runs up north and greater revenue for me, while strengthening my position with suppliers on their behalf."

Joshua says he'd time orders from dealers so that he could lump several deliveries together and make one long trip. It meant that he was carrying upwards of 200 pounds or more of pot. On such deliveries, he'd hire people to drive what he called "chase and scout cars," one driving ahead to spot speed traps and other police activity, the other behind to make sure he wasn't being followed by someone looking to rip him off. These runs would include "multiple" individual stops from Vermont and Maine, all the way south to Virginia Beach.

Joshua made numerous runs over several months, pocketing at least $5,000 per; and frequently, much more than that. At the time, he owned a veritable arsenal of weapons. Along with the two 9mm Berettas, and a .38 Smith & Wesson revolver, among his favorites were a 9mm Austrian Glock 18; a SIG-Sauer P228; his "heavy hitter," a Smith & Wesson .357 Magnum; and his "trophy piece," the German-made MP5K 9mm submachine gun, which featured a 30-round magazine and cost Joshua $5,200. But he had the money to spend. The guns, the truck, his leather jacket and tens of thousands of dollars' worth of crystal-meth and cocaine for personal use were funded by his transportation business. His life was fast and furious, the kind of existence that has no shelf life. At 20, Joshua's life expectancy, or at least his freedom, was terminal. If a rival dealer or his out-of-control drug use didn't get him, the cops would. As it happened, it was the last of those three options that ended his marijuana transportation career.

In the late summer of 2001, police pulled over Joshua's Silverado on U.S. 13, a main drag through Virginia's Eastern Shore. Headed to his final delivery in Virginia Beach, he was carrying less than five pounds of marijuana and an undisclosed amount of cocaine on him when he was stopped. He and an associate riding in the truck with him were arrested, and appeared before a magistrate. Joshua was able to arrange a secure bond, and was released with a trial scheduled in April of 2002. He wouldn't make that court date. By then, he'd already be in jail in Connecticut facing a 30-year prison sentence.

Joshua's exit from marijuana transportation came "quickly and decisively," he says. He was forced to retire his position in the trade because of his arrest, he wrote.

I had to drop my contacts . . . once you missed a re-up you out of the loop and no longer privy to the

next date, location and time of the next meet, it's a
fail-safe for the supplier, if you couldn't maintain for
what ever reason, you were a liability.

Though Joshua is businesslike in his description of his departure from the trade as if the decision had been prudent and thought out, the truth of the matter is, he was running out of time. He had shot his quicksilver fortune into his veins and, he's quick to add, "up nostrils of my friends' noses." He had a court date pending in Virginia, but that would prove to be the least of his problems.

By this time, Joshua had moved to Bristol, Connecticut, and into an apartment with a girl he was seeing. He was broke now, but drugs were available "in varied abundance." The apartment was a crash pad and smoking parlor, Joshua would write:

It wouldn't have mattered what seat you sat in
anywhere in the apartment a smoking piece of some
type was within easy reach and multi-chambered bongs
were on accessible display like trophies won in a smok-
ing marathon.

Out of the apartment in Bristol, Joshua became something of a local "specialized" drug dealer. He sold ecstasy, including "triple stack," which had three times the dosage in a single pill. One of the drugs he sold was "Special K." Ketamine, developed by Parke-Davis for both human and veterinary use, produces a feeling of anesthetic disassociation, and short-term hallucinations. He would buy the "K" in liquid form in brown glass vials. He would then drip the liquid onto glass platters and place them in the oven for a couple of minutes until they crystallized. Once the platters were removed from the oven and cool, he would use a razor blade to scrape the hardened ketamine into small piles of powder to be packaged and sold.

Though he ingested his own share of Special K, he was especially susceptible to the drug: "never did have a high tolerance for it," he says.

But if his Special K capacity was less than prodigious, he was an acid freak of monumental proportions. His connection was a local "chemist," he says. So potent was this LSD, packaged in clear glass beakers, he would cut it with grain alcohol. Joshua describes his deliveries at this time like a scene from *Who Framed Roger Rabbit*. "Tripping his balls off," as he describes it, he would drive the Silverado through the streets of Bristol, which became a Toontown. The truck would float over the pavement like a hovercraft, the road in its headlights rippling and buckling in front of him.

Joshua liked to drop acid during camping trips, and while 4×4ing in his Silverado. He tripped while attending raves in the woods, gatherings replete with pulsating "techno music" and strobe and laser light shows. One time he almost freaked when he came upon an abandoned hunting cabin with a girlfriend. The paint on the cabin's walls seemed to peel off right before his eyes. One of Joshua's favorite stops in Bristol was LSD Point, "a semi-secluded lookout above the town, so called because the street lights below spelled out these three magical letters in proper order (Evidently, the lights spelled out "LSD")." One time he was there at the Point with a girlfriend named Sarah. Joshua recounted the moment much later in a letter from jail:

Sarah was holding her own as we were parked up there in the darkness, the rain falling, my truck run-

ning idly, the little lights of dashboard electronics re-
flecting hues of green on the inside of the windshield,
windows open as our cigarette smoke dance upon the
dark night breeze. We were laid-out across the seats,
she in front and I across the back seat watching the
rain drops trickle down the windshield creating halos
of color when they exploded against the glass seem-
ingly melting and deforming . . . in such a way Dali
would be proud.

But in reality, life started to close in on Joshua. He was
AWOL from the U.S. Army. He had the court date in Virginia
pending. He was using drugs like a man who wanted to die.
He was out of money, and had very few friends.

After a few months, he moved out of Bristol and into a
condominium in nearby Southington. It was while living in
Southington that Joshua met a man who used drugs in the
same suicidal way that he did.

Like Steven Hayes, the man I'll call Uncle Joe was quite a
bit older than Joshua, but shared the same appetite for shooting cocaine. They would go together on drug binges that
would last for days, shooting sugar water every now and then
to keep their bodies from collapsing.

One time Joe and Joshua obtained a large quantity (in
terms of personal use) of a high quality of cocaine called
"fishscale." Towards the end of the binge, maybe three or four
days after it had started, Joe announced "he was done." Joshua
thought he meant that he had used the last of the coke. Then
he watched though a coke-stoned haze as his running partner
filled a syringe with whiskey and shot it into his vein. Somehow Joe survived, but only after an I.C.U. visit that lasted
three days, and soon he and Joshua were back at it again.

CHAPTER TWENTY-NINE

Robert Louis Stevenson was said to have written *Dr. Jekyll and Mr. Hyde* as an allegory of the internal conflict between good and evil in all of us. Joshua was very familiar with Stevenson's tale, both as reader and as someone who identified with the story, writing in a letter from jail:

> *The struggle with my personal civil war battling on the grounds of my soul has created a seemingly personified Dr. Jykyll and Mr. Hyde nightmare.*

In Stevenson's story, Dr. Jekyll discovers that he has become addicted to his Hyde, and inexorably the evil in the doctor's personality takes over until Hyde dominates Jekyll. Ultimately, the doctor realizes, the only way he can stop Hyde is by killing himself.

Joshua had periods of such self-hatred that he believed his own death was his only refuge. Time and again he awoke from drug binges surprised and disappointed that he was still alive. Whether it was a hunting knife used for self-mutilation, or a hypodermic needle, or a vial filled with pills, or a revolver at his temple, from the day he wrote the suicide note after the Huxley fire, Joshua was on a quest to end his life. He believed there was something in him, an evil force, one that no amount of drugs or prayer could allay, a force that would have its way regardless of how hard he tried to keep it down. "Repression," he wrote,

> *a haunting trait that by definition enjoys its obscurity, living, slinking in the further chamber of the mind, its shadow costing years of distressing thoughts, turning the whole turmoil in my mind into congealed rage.*

But it was while living in Southington that someone would intercede in Joshua's downward plunge. There, he would meet a 15-year-old girl who made his life worth living again, a girl who would become the mother of his child.

It was early evening and Joshua was sitting in the bong water–stained living room when a girl with Halloween-black hair and eyes that looked as though they were made of sapphire sat on the arm of the recliner and leaned against him. Joshua didn't know her. Lord knows, she wasn't the only unfamiliar girl he saw in the house. The place was a regular Grand Central Station of females from every walk of life.

By his own estimation, Joshua had multiple circles of friends, that ran the gamut from "Goths" to Christians, from hard-working construction pals to what Joshua called his "candie-flipping, acid-dropping raver" friends, and variances of each. Jennifer fell into the Goth/punk rocker category, and Joshua was smitten by what he called her "Goth standoffishness."

During one of their initial conversations, Joshua told her that she was cute. In the Goth culture, being called "cute" is an insult. "She'd get that fire in her eyes," Joshua would later write about Jennifer's anger, "scrunch-up her perfectly shaped nose and start speaking with her hands." Jennifer's gesticulations would usually end with a punch to Joshua's arm.

In the beginning of their relationship, he loved to bait her, more like a brother to his sister than a boyfriend to a girlfriend. But Joshua told friends that his relationship with Jennifer was a "Cinderella story," and that he wanted, as time with her went on, to live the rest of his life with her. "She was someone who wanted me despite my continual mistakes," he would write.

It's hard to imagine a relationship born in the party atmosphere of the house in Southington having much of a shelf life. Still, they were inseparable. "There weren't many times we were apart for longer than a few hours," Joshua wrote. Although both would admit that much of that time was spent in the condominium or at raves partying, there were also more traditional dates like dinners and movies, of which Joshua was a real buff.

Though five years younger than Joshua, who was 21, Jennifer was in a way the more mature of the two. After he had walked away from the U.S. Army, Joshua had bounced around from Southington, back to Cheshire and then to Bristol. It was during this time that he was mainlining cocaine with Uncle Joe, smoking crystal-meth and dropping so much LSD, he astounded even his acid-dropping friends—"Rarely do I come across anyone who can go drop for drop with me," Joshua wrote. But just a few weeks into their relationship, Jennifer gave Joshua an ultimatum. He remembered the exact night she'd issued the proviso. It had snowed heavily, and they had argued. Her words, according to Joshua, were simple and forceful: It's either the needle or me, she'd said. "I chose her," Joshua would write, "closing that chapter of my life."

And Joshua did make an effort to straighten up. Along with taking intravenous cocaine out of the equation (Joshua contradicts himself in a letter where he states that he went back "to using" after his arrest in Virginia), he worked a couple of jobs for contractors and such. Joshua never had problems getting work. He had plenty of skills. In the Reserves, he'd earned a military operator's license for tractor-trailers. But, as his mother would later tell a judge, he lost every job he started, one after the other, because of "his drug problems."

Though Joshua was trying to live a normal lifestyle for his girlfriend, "normal" for Joshua wasn't exactly "normal" for everyone else. He was still selling marijuana, Special K and acid, and he also began to revert to his old ways for his main source of income—a vocation that had begun when he was just 12, and one in which he would show remarkable talent.

You can categorize Joshua as a cat burglar. His trademark was entering houses at nighttime while his victims slept, a highly unusual method. Most home burglaries are committed in the daytime when the odds that no one is home are better. But what further separated Joshua from most burglars was that he would hire himself out to steal.

As a burglar for hire, he says, Joshua has been paid to furnish an entire house. With the help of several assistants and a U-Haul truck, he has stolen beds, bureaus, couches, cocktail tables, dinning room sets, home entertainment systems, a pool table, a washer/drier combo, end tables, lounge chairs, patio sets, pots, pans, silverware, refrigerator, china sets and "even a polished copper country kitchen sink ☺," he wrote. "Homeowners would come home to find their clothes on the floor and everything else missing . . . rude awakening."

Among the people Joshua says he stole for were identity thieves who paid him to break into a small insurance company to steal files that included dates of birth, Social Security and account numbers, and addresses. He burglarized a lawyer's office to steal a client's files. More than once, he broke into a veterinarian's office to steal ketamine and other drugs. He worked for drug dealers who paid him to break into rivals' homes and stash-houses to steal product, money "or just trash the place to set an example," he wrote. He was hired by a computer hacker to break into a computer store from which he stole laptops, hard drives and software. Joshua burglarized clothing stores and sporting goods stores, and even disabled the alarm and secured access for a team of thieves who broke into a dealership and stole jet skis, four-wheelers and dirt bikes.

When he worked for himself, however, Joshua seemed to be indiscriminate as to the type and size of burglary in which he engaged. Though there were times that the urge to steal prompted a quick slash of a back screen door and a dash through a home, there were other times were he took great pains in staking out his quarry. In the latter instances, he would check for dog runs, security motion lights and kid toys, and the age group for which those toys were designed. He would note the number of vehicles, the comings and goings of people in the house, the type of alarm system. He would check to see if the windows were double hung, casement, crank or slider, for each posed their own unique obstacles. He would note the type of exterior doors and type of locks. He would take special care in ascertaining the sight lines of the house.

There were times he would stand in the shadows of a yard for hours observing. He would become familiar with the surroundings of his target: the sidewalks, streetlights and even the storm drains of the neighborhood. He says that he escaped a police cruiser once by crawling into a sewer and "popping up like a gopher" on another street. Another time, he decided to abort a daytime heist when he realized that the house he was about to break into was right across the street from the neighborhood school bus stop, and its congregation of wary eyes. "Teenagers are one thing," he wrote, "grade schoolers with parental chaperons is quite another." He gave credence to such things as "neighborhood watch" programs, and would usually move on to another block to target, "though neighborhood watches are only looking for things that are out of place," he wrote, and if you look like you belong, then you are invisible.

From behind a tree line from across the street, or just leisurely walking by on a sidewalk, Joshua would memorize as much of the layout of the house as he could, he wrote:

I'd camp out on the property watching and waiting until the home owner begins their ritual of getting ready for bed. When I notice this, I walk up to the side of the window with the best line of sight of the key pad on the alarm control panel (if the house even has an alarm) and watch the owner punch in his code—everyone feels safe in their homes and never think to shield what code their punching in.

Once Joshua had the code to the alarm system, his preparation was finished. He would then take his time, maybe go out for a beer or a game of pool at a local strip joint.

At some point he'd change into his burglar outfit: nice slacks, dark in color and worn over combat boots, and dark (not black) pullover long-sleeve shirt. In cooler weather he'd wear a turtleneck sweater and a black skullcap. "I'd look like

I could be coming home from the club," he wrote. He would always have a pair of thin black leather gloves.

His tools of the trade included a lock pick set (although he says that most modern locks are pick-resistant), a small size Stanley screwdriver, AA Maglite with red lens, eighteen inches of thin steel wire, a multi-tool, and lastly, he wrote, "a double edge diving knife held in a quick release sheath strapped up-side-down to my forearm inside my sleeve."

He would return to the house when he was confident that everyone was asleep. And usually he would be inside in a matter of minutes.

Though court records state that Joshua broke into nineteen houses during 2000–2001, Joshua himself says that that figure is only "the tip of the iceberg," and that his burglaries actually numbered in the hundreds. Although he enlisted hired help for some, for the most part, he committed them alone.

He saw being a burglar as his calling, and he was at his most purposeful in the commission of these crimes. But like an addiction that needed to be fed with more risk, more brazenness each time, his burglaries would begin to swallow his life. Although common sense dictates that Joshua's motivation to burgle was his drug addiction, there is something about his burglaries that stood apart from that. He'd begun breaking into houses before he was addicted to drugs, and he contends, over and over in letters and interviews, that burglary for him was never about the money. He said that he thought of it as an extreme sport, and got off on the adrenaline rush. There is the possibility, however, that he was aroused by neither money nor adrenaline, but by a twisted desire.

* * *

The apex of Joshua's burglar career occurred during the summer of 2001. By his count, Joshua broke into scores of houses in those months. In the midst of it, that August, Joshua took Jennifer to New Hampshire. They stayed in a lakeside cabin. It was during that trip, Joshua said, that Jayda was conceived. By the time Jennifer was showing her pregnancy, Joshua had already been arrested in Virginia.

In one sense he was lucky. The arrest came at the very end of a marijuana transportation run. Had it occurred a stop or two earlier, he would have been caught with significant weight, and would not have been able to make the bond. But Joshua's luck was about to run out.

Later, in his letters from jail, Joshua would say that he'd had a feeling that Connecticut law enforcement was closing in on him. He didn't have to be clairvoyant to figure that out. It was around this time that his mother's caller I.D. had unveiled the true identity of the detective trying to pass himself off as an employee of the Motor Vehicle Department.

Joshua also suspected that a friend to whom he supplied marijuana was turning state's evidence against him after being arrested. No doubt the dealer had plenty to tell the cops about Joshua. According to court records, Joshua had burglarized at least two houses in the dealer's neighborhood, one right across the street from where the dealer lived with his parents. During that particular burglary, Joshua had taken apart a desktop computer and made two trips out to his truck with the monitor, PC tower, keyboard and printer while his victims slept soundly upstairs.

But though he knew the law was closing in, Joshua contends that all of his legal troubles paled in importance to

Jennifer's pregnancy and the prospect of becoming a father. He also says that Jennifer was "giddy" at the realization that she was about to become a mother.

Joshua didn't tell Jennifer about his mounting worries—and the louder those worries played in his thoughts, the more stoic he became. It was almost as though Joshua was living in the fantasy that his troubles would disappear, or that yet another benevolent judge would take pity and send him on another adventure. For all of his criminal exploits, Joshua had not, up until this point, spent any significant time in jail. But this time his problems would not just go away.

CHAPTER THIRTY

On December 20, 2002, Joshua, now 22, stood in front of a judge in Superior Court in Bristol, Connecticut. His countenance was contrite, his prison garb hung loosely off his slight frame and his large ears protruded from the sides of his head like those of a fifth grader. When the judge, James Bentivegna, said good morning to him, his response, "Good morning, Your Honor," sounded almost sweet. But despite his innocent appearance, Joshua's odds of beating a jail sentence this time were very slim. In fact, there was a good chance that this judge was going to send him to jail for a very long time. Joshua had already pled guilty to nineteen counts of burglary.

Joshua had sat in prison for nine months awaiting sentencing after his arrest for the burglaries. Fittingly, most of that time was spent in Cheshire Correctional Center, the jail that loomed over his hometown, and was within a few miles of dozens of houses that he'd burglarized. Most of his time in Cheshire Correctional was spent in solitary confinement—twenty-three hours a day locked alone in a cell. The unusual nature of his incarceration wasn't a form of extended punishment. According to an attorney, Joshua had overheard gang members plotting an escape, and informed on them. It's tempting to believe that Joshua was using the information as a bargaining chip to perhaps lessen his sentence—he certainly

remembered the outrage and fear Cheshire had displayed
when prisoners escaped from the jail in the mid-90s. Joshua
denies being a snitch. Months after that rainy Cheshire morning, he wrote a four-page diatribe decrying the lack of jailhouse code and courage:

> . . . the State of Connecticut is embarrassingly soft on
> inmates. They coddle and cater to them like their chil-
> dren and surprise, surprise years of liberal political
> hand-holding has bred a new breed of Ct. inmates . . .
> snitches, bitches and cowards."

But if Joshua wasn't a snitch, one has to wonder why the
Connecticut D.O.C. thought his life was at risk. If Joshua
had informed, officials had good reason to worry about his
safety. Connecticut prisons are notorious for their gang
problems. The Northeast faction of the Latin Kings had begun behind Connecticut bars. According to the U.S. Department of Justice, in 2002 there were at least four major prison
gangs operating in Connecticut, including the Latin Kings,
Los Solidos, Neta and 20 Luv, and offending any of them
was a considerable risk to personal safety. A few years earlier, gang members recognized a guard from Cheshire Correctional on a Hartford street and beat the man with pipes. A
memo was issued to all Cheshire prison guards warning of
gang-ordered hits against them. Another guard from the John
R. Manson Youth Institution, the jail where Steven Hayes
had spent significant time, was convicted of being a member
of the Latin Kings and ordering an attack on an inmate.

Prison officials not only thought Joshua's life was at
risk—so too, they believed, were those of his family, girlfriend
and daughter, all of whom received some degree of police
protection.

After nine months, the threat began to dissipate and Joshua was finally removed from solitary and allowed some gym and recreation time. He liked to play chess with a few other inmates and chat with guards, with whom he had a respectful relationship. In prison, Joshua would prove to be an ideal inmate. He stayed away from trouble and drugs. Although documentation is not available, one would assume he was administered some type of medication and/or anti-depressants (he did say he was given medication in prison after the Cheshire murders). He also attended 12-step meetings while awaiting his sentencing.

But if the gangs were no longer an issue, Joshua had a more pressing problem to keep his mind occupied. And, as he stood in front of Judge Bentivegna, he awaited that fate.

The courtroom was sparsely populated. There was no jury, as this was a sentencing hearing. Joshua was already guilty, by his own admission. In the gallery sat Joshua's mother, Jude, who once again had come to support her son in a courtroom. In spite of all of her son's failings, Jude loved Joshua as if he were her own flesh and blood. She wanted to take him by the hand, as she had done in the principal's office in Norton Elementary, and lead him right out of the courtroom. Joshua's mom knew the goodness in Joshua. She remembered the little boy who'd romped and played in the woods, the kid who'd taken care of the goats. She saw, as Joshua stood in front of the judge, the young student with insatiable curiosity. She knew in her heart that Joshua loved Jesus, and that Jesus loved him back, and that the temptation and trouble her son experienced were all just tests of faith. And she had all the faith in the world that the goodness in him would somehow prevail.

Ben Komisarjevsky too sat in the courtroom in support of

his son, putting pride and anger aside. "We do love him and care about him," Ben said to the court. But Ben was pragmatic. There were those who wondered whether Ben really believed Joshua's goodness could defeat the evil that he knew had such a hold of his son.

Joshua too knew of this evil. "The darkness," he called it, a force, he said, over which he had no control. But if Ben or Joshua couldn't control the darkness, the state of Connecticut was just about to try.

Joshua's girlfriend, Jennifer, was also in the courtroom. Asleep in her arms most of the time was Jayda, their infant daughter. Joshua had held his daughter, named after his best friend Jay, for the first time in an antechamber to the courtroom, and had exhaled a wondrous laugh as he did. Touching the little body had sent a bolt through him like an electric charge. Only once before had he felt love of this strength, the afternoon in a bedroom in a condo in Southington when Jen, seven months pregnant, fell asleep in his arms.

At 16, slender with blonde hair highlighted in purple and red (she had stopped dying her hair black), Jennifer was, chronologically at least, nearer childhood than womanhood. Joshua insists she was 16, but records show that she had been 15 at the time they met. Regardless of their age difference, Joshua insists that they were in love.

Maybe it was everlasting love. A 16-year-old mother, her hands filled with an infant, battling her own demons of addiction, she had shown up at every one of Joshua's court appearances. As his eyes locked on hers in the courtroom, he managed a little grin, and his thoughts, he would write, went to the day he had his hand on her pregnant belly:

> *I was lying there beside her knowing that soon I was*
> *to be a daddy. I was so happy yet so overcome with*

disappointment in myself, I felt so undeserving of this kind of happiness . . .

Joshua says that he didn't tell Jen that his past was quickly catching up to him. "I didn't know then how to communicate my struggle with her or her parents so I remained silent," he would write about that time.

Though Jennifer's show of support was heartfelt and even courageous, it's doubtful she fully comprehended the fix in which Joshua was about to leave her. How limiting are the prospects of a 16-year-old mother when the father of her child is about to be sentenced to years in jail? For all of Joshua's professions of love for Jennifer and Jayda, he was about to abandon them.

There are three versions of how Joshua was caught, or perhaps the three versions are ingredients to the capture.

Bill Glass was just about to retire from the Cheshire police force when he got a call one night from a friend named Ray Sirico, a meat purveyor in town. Sirico told the Cheshire cop about a suspicious truck parked on his street. Glass cruised by and ran the plate of the white Toyota pickup. A house on that block had been robbed, and the truck belonged to Joshua.

But according to Joshua's lawyer, the break in the investigation came when a trace on electronic equipment stolen from two houses in the Bristol area had led them to a local pawnshop called Easy Money, where Joshua had used his New Hampshire driver's license for identification. Joshua does confirm that he'd pawned the merchandise and used his own I.D.: "I was pressed for time and money . . ." he wrote. He was also shooting up cocaine, to take the "edge" off his stress.

But Joshua contends that the main reason he was finally caught was that a friend and marijuana business associate had used his knowledge of Joshua's criminal affairs as a "stay out of jail card."

After Connecticut police visited the pawnshop, they went to Jennifer's parents' home on Wilderness Way in Bristol. There, a search of the basement revealed items stolen out of burglarized homes that police believed had Joshua's trademark. According to Joshua, cops had been aware of his method of operation for a very long time. He singles out one Cheshire detective, Dennis Boucher, who, Joshua says, "knew the criminal side of me well." Boucher engaged in a game of "cat and mouse" with him for quite some time, Joshua wrote.

> *I have developed a style of burglary over the years that forms the frame work of all my burglaries. Boucher knows by looking at a burglarized building if it's mine or not.*

Though the relationship between cop and robber, and Joshua's reputation, might seem to have harmless elements of Inspector Clouseau and the Pink Panther, nothing could be farther from the truth. As word of the Petits' home invasion began to spread, before anyone knew the criminal actors involved, Joshua's name was the first that came to at least one retired Cheshire P.D. member: "I knew it was Komisarjevsky," said Bill Glass.

His arrest in Virginia, Joshua would later say, was the first domino to fall in a short chain of events that he knew would lead to a jail cell (Northampton County decided not to prosecute Joshua, as he was facing significant jail time in Connecticut). And when he was arrested in Connecticut, he gave in to the inevitable, he wrote:

. . . the police had warrants for a couple of counts of burglary of which I took responsibility for, then [I] confessed to 17 others they didn't know about, much to the surprise of the investigating officers!"

During a tour of the houses he'd burglarized, Joshua told the cops in precise detail his method and times of entry and exit in each. He described the insides of each house, down to the color schemes, the style of furniture, even the photographs on the wall. He listed, almost to the item, the things he'd stolen, including the exact dollar amount. Although the recovered goods represented only a fraction of Joshua's ill-gotten gains, they amounted to a veritable cross-section of merchandise that included BMX mountain bikes, crystal vases, a Mercedes-Benz hood ornament, a purse with $40, another with just $20, credit cards, drivers' licenses, 19,000 dollars' worth of electronic equipment and flatware and china. Among the items listed was a medical bag and stethoscope. Joshua told the cops that in some houses he'd spend hours roaming around, in others he was in and out in a moment.

The breadth and method of his crimes shocked even the most hardened of law enforcement officials. In his fifteen years in the D.A.'s office, preceded by eight years as a cop on the street, Prosecutor Ronald Dearstyne said that he had never encountered a burglar like Joshua.

If Joshua is to be believed, he admitted to the burglaries because of the birth of his daughter. Whatever the consequence of his crimes, Joshua wanted Jayda to someday know that her new life had prompted a new, law-abiding chapter in his. His apparent change of heart was convincing. Even the state troopers who'd driven Joshua to the crime scenes petitioned the prosecutor to show him leniency.

But the prosecution wasn't all that impressed with Joshua's confession. "This is not a situation where he woke up one day and decided, 'I've done something terribly wrong here,' got dressed, and walked down into the police department and said, 'Here I am, this is what I've done,'" said Ronald Dearstyne to the court. "He pretty much copped out to these after he was arrested on two warrants already."

Right from the start of the sentencing hearing it was obvious that Prosecutor Dearstyne wanted to put Joshua away for as much time as he could—a minimum sentence of 10 years. He argued that breaking into homes at night while people, including children and a handicapped woman who was relegated to a wheelchair, slept in bedrooms upstairs was a violation of the most dangerous and lasting kind. "A lot of people seem to think that theft and breaking into homes is a crime against property," Dearstyne said. "In fact, it's not really a crime against property; it's a crime against the people who live in those homes."

Armed with the pre-sentencing investigation, a report assembled by state police that included statements by Joshua's victims, the prosecutor had convincing material. After Joshua had burglarized their homes, at least three of his victims had gone out and bought home security systems. "I know he's locked up," said one woman about Joshua, "but I still think someone is trying to get into my house." Another of his victims told police, "Defendant should get as much jail time as possible." Still another said, "Someone like him shouldn't be out on the street." Maybe the most compelling statement by a victim, at least when the events of July 23, 2007, are taken into consideration, was the man who told police how frightened his four children were after the incident. "We were just glad that he didn't go upstairs where the kids were," the man said.

"If you can't feel safe in your own home at night," Dearstyne asked, "where can you feel safe?"

Years later, in a letter from jail, Joshua would contradict his motive for confessing his crimes to the Bristol court. He wrote that his confession was more "tactical" than anything else. He told the cops about the homes that he thought might be linked to him in the future. ". . . it was a calculated risk confessing and wasn't easy but I didn't want them [the burglaries] coming back on me," he wrote.

CHAPTER THIRTY-ONE

There's an old story about a man who gets a flat tire while driving past an insane asylum. In starting to change the tire, he takes all the lug nuts off and puts them in the hubcap for safekeeping. Just then a car speeds by and clips the hubcap, sending the lug nuts rolling down a sewer grate and out of reach. As the man is shaking a fist at the speeding car, he hears a voice behind him.

"Why don't you take one of the lug nuts off each of the other three tires? That should hold you until you get to a garage."

The man turns towards the voice, and to his astonishment finds that it belongs to an inmate behind the fence of the asylum.

"If you're so smart, what are you doing in there?" he asks the man behind the fence.

"I might be crazy, but I'm not stupid," comes the reply.

Joshua's defense counsel was William Gerace, a Hartford criminal attorney with a great deal of experience and a delivery that was polished smooth. Though eloquent, Gerace had rather an odd way of trying to elicit leniency from the judge, considering the DA's laundry list of Joshua's crimes, and how the sentences for them added up. "He should be doing thirty years," Gerace said of his client at one point. "It's a terrible thing to have your home burglarized."

Of course, Gerace knew there was no way to minimize what Joshua had done. His client was a serial burglar who had committed crimes that were of the most invasive kind. But Gerace also suspected that there was something different about this case.

When he'd taken on Joshua as a client, Gerace received a letter from him written in jail. Most of the letter was an apology for forgetting the name of Gerace's assistant counsel, with a small portion given to inquiries about his case.

Joshua's tone and mastery of the language took Gerace by surprise. It was certainly like no other defendant's letter he had received in his many years as a defense attorney. "There is something odd about this whole circumstance," Gerace would tell the court.

Gerace argued that Joshua's confession had not been an epiphany, but was proof of his client's emotional instability. "A person who can . . . name what they took and how they took it in such detail, obviously has a twisted psyche," he said. "I think it's a mental aberration of some sort . . ." Among the words and phrases Gerace would use to categorize his client included "mental abnormality," "terribly disturbing," "bizarre" and "erratic."

Gerace's oratory in front of the court was perhaps the first time Joshua's mental health history had been so publicly displayed. And stacked, one on top of the other, his psychological problems were as extensive as they were longstanding.

Any oral history of Joshua's psychosis begins with what happened in his bedroom when he was 6, but there were other physical traumas that might have caused psychological damage. According to Gerace, his family saw "a progressive personality deterioration," because of them.

As Joshua remembers it, the first of the concussions occurred when he was 9 or 10 years old. One snowy winter's day, he was riding in the back seat of the family station wagon when he took his seatbelt off ("against my parent's rules," he wrote) to reach for a toy or a book. Just then a pickup truck crossed the median and slammed into the Komisarjevskys' car head-on. Joshua was thrown into the side window and door column. "I don't remember anything after that except that there was alot of blood," he wrote.

The injury's most significant consequence, at least according to Joshua, came on the soccer field. "Whenever someone kicked the ball at my face, I would unconsciously turn my head taking my eyes off the game."

Despite a habit of flinching, Joshua was fearless when it came to activities. And injuries that resulted from his daring behavior had begun even before the car accident. He broke his arm falling from high up in one of the oak trees in front of his grandfather's house. At least two concussions had come when he was riding his mountain bike. Later in his teens, when his interest in extreme sports became an obsession, he suffered head injuries while snowboarding, rock-climbing and downhill mountain biking.

It got to the point, he says, where his parents treated his hospital visits with a certain amount of emotional detachment. "The first question they'd ask upon 'getting the call,'" Joshua would write, "is whether or not I'm still breathing—if the answer is yes, they'll say 'oh he'll be ok then' ☺."

Joshua sustained a concussion from the injuries he'd received when the gunpowder exploded in his face in New Hampshire. He had another when he flipped a pickup truck he was driving. Still another came when he was touring with the Continentals—he grabbed a charged lighting support while setting up lighting trusses and awoke in an I.C.U. Still another concussion came the day after he was released from the hospital. "I experience a dizzy spell, blacked out and fell all the way down a staircase," he wrote.

According to court records, Joshua had suffered nine concussions. But according to Joshua, you could probably double that number and come up short.

"I don't know if any of this is the reason or the cause," Gerace told the court. "I'm pointing them out because something went wrong somewhere with Josh."

It was then when Gerace brought up Joshua's stay at Elmhurst psychiatric hospital.

According to Gerace, Joshua's parents thought the medication he was prescribed at Elmhurst was a "crutch," and an indication of character weakness. He said they believed their son should "deal with it on a spiritual level." In one way, it's hard to fault the Komisarjevskys for their decision. The debate between Christianity and psychotherapy is longstanding. The two sides have stood apart in a sort of leery appraisal maybe since Darwin was pitted against Genesis in a Tennessee courtroom.

It is hard to prove a person wrong who makes decisions according to their faith, especially when community pressure is applied to that decision. The Komisarjevskys were fervent members of a Christian community and, no doubt, went to church pastors and elders for advice. They made their decision according to their faith. But they did so in spite of Joshua's long history of disappointing those who put their faith in him.

Perhaps there is no moment in the New Testament that captures the importance that Christians place on forgiveness than in the conversation between the penitent thief later named Dismas and Christ on the cross:

> *And he said unto Jesus, "Lord, remember me when thou comest into thy kingdom." And Jesus said unto him, "Verily I say unto thee, today shalt thou be with me in paradise.*[6]

More times than he could count, Joshua had asked and been granted forgiveness. In retrospect, it was almost as if he was playing a game, manipulating those filled with faith and naively credulous. It would seem that way, except that he played the game so well that it was hard not to believe that, somewhere in his heart, he was truly sorry for his deeds.

The battle between good and evil played out in Joshua as if Milton had written it. The good Christian boy, that part of him with clear eyes and a full heart, wanted nothing more but to be one with nature and search for the goodness and love in life. Over and over, Joshua collected youth pastors and Christian friends who believed that God's light shone within him. Their number precludes the possibility that Joshua could be conning all of them.

There is one youth pastor from Maine who asked to not be named in this story because of how betrayed he felt by Joshua's final act of destruction. The pastor had given Joshua many chances at redemption. Each time Joshua would raise the pastor's hopes, only to dash them by behavior that seemed as though it was motivated by evil. Even after that night in Cheshire, Mark Middlebrooks continued to believe that redemption was possible for Joshua, writing in a letter to him:

------

[6] Luke 23: 39–43

You remain a man of great promise, regardless of the turn of events and regardless of what is or isn't true about them. I know what I saw in you 10 years ago and I don't question for a moment that it still exists. Others might question it, and you might even yourself, but I don't. Nor does God.

Others just as close or closer to Joshua believed he possessed a predisposition to lie. "He was a chameleon," Joshua's best friend told the *Hartford Courant*. "He showed the face he wanted you to see. If he was with his prison buddies, he was the hardest-ass prisoner there was. If he was with church people, he'd be saying 'Praise Jesus!' "

But there is also the possibility that within Joshua exists two truths: one good and one bad. He readily admits to "scoring high" on tests for schizophrenia. That condition can be explained, as Gerace tried in front of the court, in clinical terms. It can be treated with drugs and psychoanalysis. But it also can be explained in allegory and parable. Though Joshua was not stupid, not by a long shot, he struggled with the question of whether he was crazy, or if the cause of inner conflict, an urge to do what was wrong, was coming from a dark place that he had been taught as a Christian to fear. As he would later write:

I knew there was something different about me. So plainly evident on the nights when my restless inner torment would come upon me, a confusion so similar to a madness born from desperation closing in around me like a straitjacket. At times I really contemplated my own sanity. I knew I didn't really belong anywhere, drawn to my own world, dark and mysterious, where nothing is as it seems.

Joshua is also acutely aware of the dichotomy he embodies on a more corporal level. On one hand he's boastful about his life of crime:

I'm a criminal, with a criminal mind, drawn by risk and fast money.

He is also aware of how that choice of lifestyle robbed him of fulfilling his potential:

Clearly I've made bad judgement calls in my life, but I've also done a lot of good, selflessly, to better the lives of people around me.

Charming, articulate and handsome, Joshua had character traits to go just as far as life would take him:

I have an innate ability to do quite well for myself when I apply my mind and body to the task at hand whether it be recreational, academic, occupational, socially, and yes criminally.

But though on the surface Joshua might have had great potential, underneath he possessed an emotional and psychological make-up that sabotaged every positive step in his life and seemed destined to bring harm to him and others.

Joshua told the court that he truly regretted his actions. "I wish I could tell them [the victims] I'm sorry," he said. "I can't even imagine how violated. I wish there was more I could do."

Joshua's statement of guilt was part of the sentencing transcript. It was straightforward, unemotional and, given his later description of the scope of his criminal exploits, attenuated.

In the statement, he wrote that he'd begun breaking into houses when he 14 years old and that he'd always committed his burglaries during the nighttime. He stated that the only reason he'd stopped was that he'd been caught (we know now he meant caught setting the Huxley fire). He wrote that he'd always acted alone, and that all the houses he'd robbed in his teens were in Cheshire. He stated that he'd "started up again due to lack of money and a job." He briefly described his method of operation, writing that he'd always used gloves (except in the first house that he burglarized), that he'd "acquired" night vision goggles from a friend who had stolen some of his military equipment, and that he'd carried a backpack of tools, including knives that he used to cut screens. He wrote that he'd always avoided contact with people.

It wasn't William Gerace's place to try to argue his client's innocence. He was representing Joshua at a sentencing hearing. His job was simply to try to persuade the judge to be as lenient as possible. And the lawyer was cautious in his assessment of Joshua's chances: "If Joshua is truly remorseful," Gerace said at one point during the proceedings, "and is truly changing the way he acts, and the way he behaves, that's great, but I have a feeling, Judge, he's either going to be a career criminal or never come back here again."

For his part, Dearstyne didn't seem to care about Joshua's struggles with good and evil, or his sanity. And he didn't seem moved by Joshua's apology. In fact, the prosecutor's response to Joshua's statement was rather direct: ". . . of course, he has no understanding of how violated these people feel in their own homes," the prosecutor said. "These people now have to live with what happened in their home every day."

At one point, the contention between prosecutor and defendant became evident. In a statement made in the pre-sentencing investigation report, Joshua accused Dearstyne of making derisive comments towards him. "I keep hearing from the prosecutor that I'm a wild animal," Joshua wrote. "I'm not." Dearstyne took a moment in front of the judge to address the comment, denying that he'd called Joshua a wild animal. ". . . that terminology would be wrong," he said. "On the other hand, I do think he is a dangerous person who poses a danger to the people of the state of Connecticut, and, as a result, should be punished severely for what he's done here."

The prosecutor asked the court to impose a sentence of "30 years suspended after 10 years to serve." Joshua had already been sentenced in Meriden, Connecticut, for five burglaries, and had received a 3-year sentence. If Dearstyne had had his way, Joshua would have been getting out of jail about the same time as Michaela Petit was graduating from college.

CHAPTER THIRTY-TWO

Joshua stood in front of the judge and began to cry. A bailiff brought a tissue. "That's all right," the judge comforted. "Take your time." Joshua's voice cracked as he began:

"I don't know why, but I always thought that I could—that I'd be able to do everything on my own. I've turned my back on my faith in God and my family. And, in doing so, I fell flat on my face and deep into hard drugs and eventually led— eventually deepened my depression. I only pray that I have the opportunity to be able to raise my daughter in the love and the faith that now has new meaning to my life."

It was a powerful plea, delivered with his infant daughter just a matter of feet from the judge. No doubt Judge Bentivegna looked at Jayda in that moment and back to the contrite man-child standing in front of him. It is, even if only on the printed transcript of the proceedings, a poignant moment. "And I also respectfully and humbly ask," Joshua continued, "if I could turn around and express my apologies in your court to my parents in front of everyone."

Jude Komisarjevsky sat with eyes glazed with tears and nodded back to her son. Within their faith, the Komisarjevskys had tried their best with Joshua. She knew that sometimes the Lord's reasons were not revealed here on earth. But faced with the reality of Joshua's situation, Ben and Jude sought a compromise between their faith and the psychiatric field. Joshua's parents had asked their lawyer to petition the judge to consider a faith-based, two-year, in-patient treatment center as an alternative to jail. When Ben Komisarjevsky was given his say, he told the court that it was Joshua's first time behind bars, and how difficult jail was for his son. "I'm not too sure that incarceration will benefit him for a long period of time, like it hasn't for many individuals," Ben said. "It will give him more depression, I feel." This alternative to jail, Ben pled, would give Joshua a better shot at rehabilitation. "That will further his ability to come out of his depression and out of his difficulties," he said.

Relatively young for a Superior Court judge, James Bentivegna was just 37 at the time of Joshua's sentencing hearing. He had been nominated to the bench just a few months before by then–Connecticut Governor John Rowland, for whom he had worked as a legal counsel. His résumé also included a term as a family support magistrate, where he had, no doubt, presided over the worst of family situations. He had also worked as a public defender in Wisconsin, and perhaps he still retained some of that idealism of his youth. But as the judge began to deliver his sentence, his road to the bench dissolved into the moment that now solemnly enveloped his courtroom.

"It's a very unfortunate past that you've had," Judge Bentivegna began. "You've had some difficult times. It's very apparent that you have a loving family that has done as much as they can to support you, and that, unfortunately, you were subject to abuse when you were younger, and I think, for whatever reason, didn't get the treatment or counseling that you needed at that point, and that that had a factor in your committing these crimes.

"But . . ."

It was at the "But" that Joshua knew he had run out of chances. He stood there, the tears in his eyes icing to a sheen, as his feelings began to recede to a colder place.

"What those crimes show is sort of an M.O.," the judge continued. "That you would case these homes and that you would commit calculated burglaries at night while people were there sleeping . . . is somebody who is a predator, a calculated, cold-blooded predator . . . that decided that nighttime residential burglaries was your way to make money."

For Joshua, the judge's words now seemed to float in mid-air, like word balloons in a comic strip. They meant nothing to him, for they were based on nothing. It wasn't primarily the cash or the drugs that had driven him to break into houses. Joshua's motives were far more frightening. Maybe it was a sense of dominion that he never felt in his own skin or his own home. Joshua says that it was around the time he began breaking into houses when he realized that people treated him differently because he was adopted. It was then, he says, when he started to feel like he didn't belong. In the homes he burglarized, Joshua liked looking at family photographs. He liked to listen to the rhythmic breathing of strangers sleeping in their bedrooms. For Joshua these sights and sounds brought some type of satisfaction—or the promise of satisfaction.

There was also no safety in the rooms of his childhood, and he felt betrayed by those who promised safety: the Church, his parents. "His personal marionette," is how he described his relationship with his childhood abuser. The remembrance of that time disturbed him. Joshua would write about the abuse:

> *Everyone has their dues to pay in life. Life started collecting early from me. I don't want or need anyone's*

sympathy, there is not many faster ways to get on my bad side then by pitying me. I hate it. I find it degrading. I can count on one hand how many people I've opened up to about it and still have fingers to spare to flip life my middle finger.

Untreated, the fear and hurt of his childhood trauma had progressed into a subtle fury. So too did his burglaries progress in their brazenness. With each, he drew closer to the breath of those in the bedrooms, as if he were embarked on a ceaseless hunt to even an old score.

Joshua gently pushed open Hayley's door. He remembers that the color scheme of Petit's oldest daughter's bedroom was a dark blue. He focused on the silhouette of the girl sleeping in the bed. He crept up beside her, with Hayes now in the doorway blocking the little light from the hall.

"And, as the state indicated," the judge continued, "a number of these people are so fearful now after having suffered what happened that they had to get alarm systems, and they feel very uncomfortable being in their own homes."

Down the hall, Joshua took Michaela from her mother's arms and led her to her bedroom. He remembers Michaela wearing orange pajama bottoms and a yellow tee shirt.

"I think it's fair to characterize your course of conduct as predatory," Judge Bentivegna said.

The room was filled with stuffed animals, he remembers, "like a zoo." A room where little girl's secrets were kept in a diary, where imagination bloomed like the pastel colors on the walls, where the future was filled with wonder and all the stories in her books ended happily.

"In terms of— in weighing what the proper sentence would be, I need to determine what's necessary to provide just punishment . . . I also need to determine what's necessary to protect the public by isolating you from society for some period of time."

He had a cell phone with a camera, just like the one he'd used to take pictures of Caroline.

"I also have to consider the goal of specific deterrence," Bentivegna continued, "to make sure that you understand that once you're released from custody, that you cannot commit these crimes any longer, and that there's going to be consequences if you do."

He tied her hands and feet and smiled a comforting smile. Her hair was pulled back into a ponytail. His brown eyes were soft and warm. He told her not to be scared, like a big brother promising his little sister he would protect her from the bogeyman. Her eyes filled with tears.

"So the total effective sentence is nine years' imprisonment in the custody of the commissioner of correction, six years' special parole. And that sentence is to run concurrent to the Meriden sentence.

". . . what that means is, for the next—basically the next fifteen years of your life, from twenty-two to thirty-seven, you're going to be either incarcerated or on special parole.

So, if you can't change your life around in the next seventeen years, there's really no hope for you."

Please don't hurt my family, Jennifer Petit pleaded.

The date was December 20, 2002. If Joshua served the entire sentence, he would be behind bars until 2011. Under Connecticut law, he was eligible for parole when he had served 50 percent of his sentence.

Joshua was a model prisoner, but whether or not he was a perfect candidate for rehabilitation was extremely debatable. There exists a 47-page transcript of Joshua's sentencing hearing, a document that is now easily found online, but one that somehow did not find its way into the hands of the parole board that would review and ultimately approve Joshua's release just four-and-a-half years after he was sentenced. A provision of his parole allowed for his electronic monitoring device to be removed on July 21, 2007.

Joshua contends that he began breaking into houses again to help a halfway house buddy out of a jam. But there had to be something in it for him, an aberrant desire, perhaps born in the bedroom of his childhood, and intensified with each house that he broke into and one that would be satisfied in the middle of the night on July 23, 2007, on Sorghum Mill Drive.

PART III

THE MURDERS

CHAPTER THIRTY-THREE

Night had become morning outside the house on Sorghum Mill Drive though the difference was barely perceptible. Dawn came wet and gray and, as the morning hours crept by, the sound of the neighborhood stretching awake, garage doors opening, cars pulling from driveways, was muted by the shroud of the dreary day. It was a rainy Monday and no one, except those kept captive inside the Petit home, could have imagined it was any different than all of the rainy Mondays that had come before.

Joshua peeked from the front bedroom window of the house as Hayes led Jennifer Petit by the arm into the Pacifica. Raindrops now bounced off the minivan and driveway. A car drove slowly by on Sorghum Mill Drive. Joshua let the curtain fall back into place. His lips were pulled tight against his teeth.

By this point, Joshua had had it with his partner. He had spent nearly six hours in the Petit house with this numbskull. First he gets lost! They had found gallon plastic jugs filled with windshield-wiper fluid in the garage. They'd emptied them and Hayes took the Pacifica out to fill them with gas. But he couldn't find his way back to the house. "He had to call three times," Joshua remembers. And then he takes off his latex gloves! Joshua had come down the stairs from Michaela's room and saw him. "Do you know what you touched?!" Joshua had screamed. He'd been all over the house, like on a treasure hunt, pulling open drawers, rooting through closets. When Joshua yelled at him, Hayes just shrugged and screwed up his face in that stupid expression of his.

Maybe it was after that that Joshua had decided, "I'm going to have to kill him." Joshua meant it too. He didn't know quite how or when, but Hayes was going to have to die. "I didn't have any problem with it," Joshua would later say.

But first, he was going to come out of this business with something to show for it. And for that, he would need his partner a little longer.

It was Joshua's idea about the bank. Had to be. Hayes didn't have that kind of imagination. Ten grand. Easy money. And Jennifer Petit would comply. According to Joshua, she'd already said as much. But he would have to send Hayes to the bank with Jennifer. Joshua figured there was too big of a chance of him being spotted by someone he knew. And, anyhow, there was something he wanted to take care of alone in the house.

It was around 8:30 a.m., and pouring rain outside. Joshua had already called his job to say he wouldn't be in, using Jayda as an excuse. He also had Jennifer Petit call her husband's office, so no one would raise the alarm.

Months later, in a jailhouse interview, Joshua would have a whole theory about Dr. Petit. Finding him on the couch had led Joshua to wonder whether there were marital problems in the Petit household. He also questioned why (according to Josh) the doctor didn't at least try to escape. He said Dr. Petit had had plenty of opportunity to do so. At one point, just before dawn, Joshua and Hayes were both out of the house for at least fifteen minutes. They'd needed to move Joshua's Venture, which was still parked in front of a neighbor's home just down the street. Driving the Petits' Pacifica,

Hayes followed Joshua to the Quarry Village condominium complex at the end of Mountain Road, 1.6 miles from Sorghum Mill Drive. "When we came back I was shocked he was still there," Joshua remembers.

Joshua's theory, however, discounts the fact that he had severely beaten Dr. Petit with a baseball bat and the very real possibility that the doctor couldn't think rationally and might not have been aware that both Joshua and Hayes were out of the house. What we do know for sure is that when Joshua and Hayes returned, Dr. Petit was still tied up in the sunroom. And Joshua had other thoughts occupying his mind, like what he was going to do with Hayes, and how he was going to get out of this house for good.

Outside the Bank of America branch, Hayes sat behind the wheel of the Petits' Pacifica as the van's wipers swept the rain from the windshield. Through the bank's front window, he watched Jennifer Petit intently, making sure she didn't try something brave. On his lap was a cell phone. Jennifer knew what the cell phone signified. She knew that the lives of her family were at stake.

Jennifer had shown amazing courage throughout the ordeal. The worst thing, she knew, was to show fear. And she tried her hardest not to. She already had hurried through the rain to the bank, but the front door was still locked. She had to go back and sit with her captor, this gruff, ugly man, for ten, fifteen minutes while they waited for the bank to open.

Around them, in the Maplecroft Plaza parking lot, Cheshire began to come to life on this dreary Monday morning. Hayes was nervous, and when he was nervous, he giggled. Why isn't the fuckin' bank open? he said as if it were a punchline for a joke. Undoubtedly, Jennifer reassured him that it would all work out fine. There are blogs filled with Cheshire Academy students' testimony of Jennifer's reassurance in their own times of trouble. It's what she did. She was a nurse, a mother.

Hayes had already taken Jennifer's pearl necklace, whatever cash the Petits had on hand and even Michaela's coins, and dropped them off in his truck, which was still parked in front of Stop & Shop. Jennifer didn't care about those things. She didn't care about the money she was about to take out of the bank. She'd take out more than they wanted—$15,000. She told both of them, the one named Josh and this one, Steven, that she understood their motive, that it had never seemed fair to her that some people didn't have to struggle for money while others did. She would give them what they wanted, and promise that she wouldn't say a word about it to anyone. When she finally saw the bank manager open the door, when Steven gave her the final orders and warning, she was glad to follow his directions so this nightmare would end.

Debbie Biggins was at the bank to open a checking account. She remembers that the clock in her car read 9:14 a.m. The bank had opened late, probably because of the heavy rain. She also told reporters that she remembered a tall, blonde woman filling out a white slip that she thought was a deposit slip. Biggins would further say that she'd known something was wrong, that she'd sensed fear. "I could feel it," she said.

Whether or not the thought occurred to Jennifer to stay in the safety of the bank, just have them call the cops, no one will ever know. But if she entertained that notion even for a moment, it was just as quickly stifled. She knew her girls were tied to their beds. There's a good chance she knew about the gallon containers of gasoline. And Joshua was home with her daughters.

I should have never talked to her, Joshua would later say.

"I liked her." In that same jailhouse interview he would slip and call Jennifer Petit "my mom." He even said she'd offered to make breakfast for him and Steven. But Jennifer Petit never lost sight of where she was and what was happening to her family.

She wanted to trust Joshua, of course she did. Why wouldn't she want him to be telling the truth when he said he wasn't going to harm her daughters? And, as it's been shown so many times, Joshua was charismatic. He had those easy-to-trust soft brown eyes. But somewhere along the line, Jennifer stopped trusting him, if she ever did. She was a pediatric nurse. She knew what a troubled child looked like. And maybe more than anything else, that's what Joshua was—a troubled child. A troubled child in a man's body who had Hayley and Michaela tied to their beds.

Jennifer Petit needed to get back to her family.

As Joshua looked down at the 11-year-old, he was surprised by her maturity. "She had a body like Caroline," he would later say in a disturbing, off-handed way. In hindsight the pieces fit so neatly. With Caroline's departure to Arizona, he'd gone from sex just about every night to none at all. Then, in the playground with Jayda that afternoon, he'd met the waitress's daughter who he thought was flirting with him. And then, just a few hours earlier, Caroline had called, and the ultimately unsatisfying cyber sex ensued.

What was Joshua looking for in all the houses that he had entered? What was it about the family photographs that interested him so? Why did he spend hours listening to the breathing coming from the upstairs bedrooms?

Joshua slid the 11-year-old's arms and legs from their bindings. Then he pulled off Michaela's pajamas, first the tops, then the bottoms. His plan, he would later say, was to extort

Dr. Petit with photos of his naked daughter. He positioned Michaela and brought the camera closer to her body. But now he released himself from his pants and began to stroke. Michaela was silent, Joshua says. She just turned her head away.

On the back of the deposit slip, Jennifer wrote a note. And, according to *The New York Times*, she also told the teller that she needed the money because her family was being held hostage, and if the police were notified, her family would be killed. Debbie Biggins saw the bank manager take the note, then peek through the blinds of her office. Jennifer hurried out the door and into the rain. She didn't want this Steven to become suspicious.

Joshua led Michaela down the hall to the shower. He told her to wash herself thoroughly. He stood there and watched. When she'd dried herself, he told her to put her pajamas back on and walked her back to bed, where he again tied her arms and legs to the posts. Then he went into Hayley's room.

Several times over the course of the last six or so hours, he had caught Hayley trying to escape. Once he'd found her with a cell phone trying to text a friend or call 911. He'd needed Steven Hayes's help to wrestle the phone from her and get her tied back to the bed. Throughout the ordeal, her eyes flashed at him in defiance. "She was a fighter," Joshua would later say.

It is not clear if Hayley knew what Joshua had just done to her sister. What is known is that the sisters' relationship was extremely close, and that Hayley was protective of Michaela.

When Joshua looked in on her, Hayley was still immobilized with the clothesline—or so it seemed to him. Regardless of how scared she must have been, Hayley was not going to let these men hurt her family any more than they already had. She had both the courage and determination to try to stop them—a "Hayley ten" of the most consequential proportion. As soon as Joshua left her bedroom, Hayley began working to free herself from the clothesline.

CHAPTER THIRTY-FOUR

According to records, the bank manager called 911 at exactly 9:21. The call took approximately four or five minutes to complete. Several times the dispatcher put the bank manager on hold, then, back on the line, more questions were asked. And more answers were given. What it was exactly that the emergency operator was asking is not known at this writing, as the released transcript was heavily redacted. But the number of questions is known: Twenty-five. Twenty-five questions and twenty-five answers. Meanwhile the Pacifica was heading back to Sorghum Mill.

Chances are, Hayes took Cornwall Avenue, the back way to the Petit home. The Pacifica flew past Edwards Road, then Oak Avenue heading towards Mountain Road. Jennifer was less than a mile from home.

The bank manager was told to hang up and call back on a direct line to police headquarters, where more questions were asked.

The Pacifica turned onto Sorghum Mill Drive.

9:26 a.m. The first radio dispatch of an "incident" at 300 Sorghum Mill Road comes on the air. At that very moment, a Cheshire police cruiser is on Higgins Road, only a minute or two away from the Petit home. The drive from the Bank of America branch to the Petit home takes approximately seven minutes. By the above calculations, the cruiser should have been at 300 Sorghum Mill Drive either just before or at the same time the Pacifica wheeled into the driveway. But for a reason that is not yet known, the police cruiser missed that opportunity.

The transcript of the second call, when the bank manager was told to call police headquarters, is a matter of public record. That document, also heavily redacted, captures the subsequent radio communication between Cheshire police and the dispatcher. Eighteen pages long, the transcript covers a time period of about thirty-five minutes, or two minutes a page.

9:34 a.m., page 4 of the transcript: The first mention of the Petit address, along with the words "HQ to all units." Moments later, several other police vehicles, both cruisers and unmarked cars, are speeding towards Sorghum Mill Drive. Interactions between cops and dispatcher are numerous, clipped and in the numerical lexicon of the Cheshire police.

9:36 a.m. A uniformed officer is out of his vehicle and approaching "the 29" (the location) on foot from Hotchkiss Ridge, a small road that loops behind the Petit home. Thinking that he might have arrived at the location before the Pacifica, the officer radios for the house number and a description "so I can, you know, see if, when, these eighteens [Cheshire police code for persons] pull up." At this point a cop on foot is literally in the Petits' backyard.

9:36–9:42 a.m. Over the next four to six minutes, the shift commander, "A1," along with the dispatcher, direct cruisers to the Bank of America branch, and coordinate roadblocks on Sorghum Mill Drive. An officer in headquarters is asked to bring a bag of his "gear" out to the location. In fact, there are several interactions about gear, rifles and helmets, and how they could be delivered to the scene.

Inside the house, neither Joshua nor Steven Hayes were aware of the police. All Joshua knew was that this marathon had to come to a close. It was now around 9:30; he'd been in the Petit home for close to seven hours. He was exhausted. It was hard enough keeping an eye on four hostages, but he also had to keep Hayes in line, especially now that there was significant cash involved. He was upstairs when he heard Hayes come into the house. He again looked in on Hayley. Then he headed downstairs. As he did, all control dissolved.

9:42 a.m. Police realize that the "white and beige vehicle" is parked in the driveway at 300 Sorghum Mill Drive. The cops' description of the Pacifica includes the mention of a "badge on the back." Dr. Petit was a member of the Hundred Club of Connecticut, a charity that cares for the surviving spouses of cops and firefighters who've lost their lives in the performance of their duty. Meanwhile, police cruisers and unmarked cars continue to race to Sorghum Mill. The shift commander is asked if the "SRT" (Special Response Team) van should be "fired up." His answer is affirmative. Cheshire's SWAT is on the way. The roadblocks on Sorghum Mill are tightened to Nutmeg Place a couple of hundred yards to the south of the Petit home and Burrage Court approximately the same distance to the north. Great pains are being taken to secure a perimeter.

9:44 a.m. An officer requests permission to try to make contact with the Petit house. "I have two phone numbers," he says in his transmission. But according to the *Hartford Courant*, no calls are made. In that same radio transmission, the officer says he has "Trooper One," the state police helicopter, "willing to go up in the air." Later on that page, the same officer says he's ordered the helicopter into the air "just in case." Again, the officer on foot behind the Petit home comes onto the air: "Uh, if you like I can approach it [a neighboring house] from the back side and attempt to make contact." The response to the officer's question, at least on paper, is terse: "Look, hold off on the contact, I just wanna see if the garage is open or anything like that . . . I just wanna make sure we have enough bodies before we start making contact."

There is a widely circulated photograph of the Petit family, taken not too long before the events of July 23. It is the perfect family photo, one that exudes togetherness, love and safety. Jennifer Petit is in the middle of the picture, flanked by her family, Michaela, Hayley and her husband. Mrs. Petit's hair is blond and wavy as it falls on either side of her long and angular face. Her smile is easy and genuine. Her eyes are slightly almond-shaped and seem to hold a bemused expression, as if the photographer's attention embarrassed her. Michaela, with a braces-dappled smile, seems to lean her head against her mother's shoulder.

Months later, Joshua would write:

I remember the look of fear, the tear rolling down the cheek, the sight of pain, the spray of blood. The sound of a tremble in a voice . . .

He says he stood on the stairs and watched as Mrs. Petit begged for her life. "Please don't kill me," she had said, the words squeaking from her throat as she ran out of breath. Hayes's hands were vise-like around her neck. According to Joshua, Hayes raped and strangled Mrs. Petit, and left her body, clothing ripped, propped against the couch. Then Hayes, his face red and maniacally stretched, looked at Joshua and smiled.

"Fuck," is all Joshua could say.

9:55 a.m. The scene outside the Petits' home is incomprehensible. On this quiet block, lined with well-appointed houses and landscaped lawns, there are now at least a dozen emergency vehicles. Most are police cars, cruisers and unmarked, their sirens quiet, and their drivers with hands clenched like fists on the steering wheels. More officers, uniformed and plainclothes detectives, some of them carrying rifles and shotguns, take up positions around the house. They follow protocol. The perimeter is secure. No one outside the house knows that one hostage is already dead.

The steady rain mutes the crackle of police radios, and hushes shouts. A man staggers in the backyard of the house at 300 Sorghum Mill Drive. "We have an eighteen somewhere out," blares the transmission. "Sounds like he's outside, somebody's outside anyhow." It is Dr. Petit. Obviously disoriented, there is a large bruise across the side of his forehead; his feet are bound with plastic ties.

The fumes from the gasoline now permeate the house. A match is lit. For a moment the flare of it reflects in Joshua's irises. Then the gas ignites with a sound like a loud clap.

A neighbor hears a scream coming from inside the Petit house. 911 calls flood the dispatcher. "We're doing what we can," one officer yells to a neighbor who has come out in their yard to see. Someone smells smoke. The tension holds. Then hell breaks.

* * *

In a full sprint, Joshua is first out of the house. Next comes Steven Hayes, screaming in a high-pitched insane laugh. On his head is Hayley's gray-and-green school hat. Tires on police cars squeal. A Cheshire police Crown Vic bolts into the driveway to block the Pacifica into which the parolees now climb. But the minivan tears across the front lawn, and as it does, chunks of grass and dirt fly from under its spinning tires. The Pacifica jumps the curb, squeals onto the street and barrels towards the roadblock one hundred yards south near Burrage Court.

The roadblock has two cop cars positioned in a V. The Pacifica gains speed as it heads right for the point of them. The crash is spectacular, a glass and metal explosion. It is followed by the groan of twisted metal and officers' shouts: "Get on the fucking ground!" The lights from the emergency vehicles slice the liquid air. A half-dozen or more cops descend on Joshua and Hayes. Knees in his back, hands pushing his face into the tar of the street, Joshua remembers how spittle had flown from the angry lips of his captors.

Less than a mile from his grandfather's estate and the Huxley garage—"I love fire," he would say, "It has a life of its own"; less than a mile from his immediate neighbor, the girl who was sure Joshua was in her room; just a little over a mile from Cheshire Correctional Institution, Joshua's criminal career has come to an end. But his final act of destruction continues.

10:01 a.m. A dozen sets of eyes are trained on the two men now cuffed and prone. A couple of hundred yards to the south an emergency worker comes on the air with a signal fifty: "C-two Cheshire . . . we have a report of a, uh, structure fire . . ."

Like the devil's tongue, flames protrude from the first-floor window and lick upwards on the front of the house. Firefighters break down the front door. The living room is an inferno. The smoke in the stairway is thick and black. The only sound the house emits is the crackling of what the fire consumes.

CHAPTER THIRTY-FIVE

Two weeks later. The smoke-stained house on the corner of Sorghum Mill Drive and Hotchkiss Ridge is cordoned off with yellow crime-scene tape. The fire did extensive damage, and plywood sheets cover the front door and windows. The Petit home is a kind of ghoulish destination. A steady stream of cars, some with out-of-state license plates, roll slowly by. The occupants of these cars are met with the steely glare of neighbors, and a discernible chill that emanates, like an icy draft, from the house itself. The rock garden on the front lawn overflows with flowers put there by friends and strangers alike. Someone has placed a statue of the Virgin Mary in the garden, but the Holy Mother's guardianship has come too late.

Whether the murders came at the hands of Steven or Joshua or both has not yet, as of this writing, been proven in a court of law. What is known, from the medical examiner's report, is that Jennifer Petit was raped and strangled. What is known is that the fire was started by gasoline. What is known is that the gasoline was poured on Jennifer Petit's body, on the stairs to the second-floor landing, around Hayley's bed into Michaela's room.

Firefighters and emergency workers who broke through the front door described the stairs as a "river of fire." Though the blaze in Michaela's room wasn't as intense as in other parts of the house, it was enough to kill her. According to the medical examiner, Michaela died of smoke inhalation, still strapped to her bed. There were also reports that gasoline was poured on Hayley, and that she suffered severely. But she was not found tied to her bed, but on the second-floor landing. Hayley escaped her ties, but succumbed to the fire and smoke, and died outside Michaela's room.

Dr. Petit managed to get out of his burning home through the basement bulkhead doors. He was transported to St. Mary's Hospital in nearby Waterbury, where he was treated for his injury and released four days later, in time to attend the funeral of his wife and two daughters.

PART IV

AUTHOR'S INTERVIEWS

CHAPTER THIRTY-SIX

Maybe it was only because of my destination—that and the fact that the day of my first trip there was overcast and gray—that I thought the town a dreary place filled with factories, train trestles and Depression-era houses. The streets have names like "Pleasant Avenue," but the feeling one gets while approaching the prison is anything but pleasant. MacDougall–Walker, the largest maximum-security prison in New England, is in Suffield, Connecticut, about a forty-five-minute drive north of Cheshire on Route 91.

The Walker building is a fairly modern brick structure. Its entrance could belong to any municipal building—except that inside, there is an immediate claustrophobic feeling. As soon as you walk through the magnetometer, you come upon a guard who sits behind a large raised and enclosed wooden desk. To the left are a few rows of molded-plastic chairs. On a wall hangs a sheet of paper that lists acceptable behavior and dress expected of visitors. It seemed to me as though the air was thinner in here, or maybe I just sensed the hopelessness.

It is in Walker where high-profile and protective-custody offenders, like Joshua, await trial.

The room in which I met him was the regular visiting room, twenty feet by thirty, lined with stools in front of Plexiglas stations. Like in the movies, there was a phone receiver next to the glass. I was alone in the room when the door slid shut behind me. When this prisoner gets a visitor, the whole building goes into a lockdown. We had the place to ourselves.

When he picked up the handset on his side of the glass, he wiped the receiver on his red prison suit, and motioned for me to do the same. The first words Joshua spoke to me were: "You can't be too careful in this place." His words were delivered with a small grin.

Polite and soft-spoken, with an easy smile, Joshua gives a likeable first impression. Of course that's not considering his surroundings and of what he's accused. He's better looking than the mug shot that was widely published after his arrest. I told him that. He said he'd been having a rough day when they took that picture. He saw me notice his fingernails, which are so long they are beginning to curl at the tips. Not allowed a nail clipper, he said.

My visit to MacDougall–Walker wasn't the first contact I had had with Joshua. I began writing to him in jail early on in the process of putting this book together. I also wrote several letters to Steven Hayes, Dr. Petit and others involved in the case. I heard nothing back from Hayes, Dr. Petit or Joshua for weeks, then months. In fact, and this is plainly an excuse, the heinousness of the crime—and the fact that as of this writing, the trial had not yet occurred—inhibited much of my reporting. Feelings were just too raw for those near to this story to talk. Then one day, after I'd just about given up hope of a response from any of them, in my mailbox was a letter from Joshua with a MacDougall–Walker Correctional Institution return address.

The handwriting on both sides of the single sheet of paper was a small, rounded-off print, like a letter from camp. He questioned my motives, but did invite me to write back. "Intelligent correspondence is at a premium here," he wrote. I did write back, a letter that contained several questions, including a rather blunt one about the sexual abuse he'd suffered as a child. "I guess there's no tactful way to ask anyone that question," he began. His answer to that question and the others I posed filled 10 pages, and so started our extended correspondence.

If Joshua was likeable in person, on paper he was fascinating. Over the next few months, we would exchange letters many times. In my first letter I'd mentioned that I heard that he was a fan of architecture. His answer was an 11-page essay on ancient Greek design that read, in my humble opinion, as though it were written by an A-student in a poly tech college—that is if there hadn't been all the smiley faces he uses to accentuate and punctuate. In fact, I was sure he'd copied it out of a text. But when I ran it through a plagiarism detection site, it came up with zero matches. He'd written it, one draft, just a few spelling errors, most of the punctuation correct and not a single cross-out. Remarkable.

Early on in our communications, I asked him to tell me his life story. Over the next few months, every two weeks or so, I would receive a new installment. In all, Joshua sent nearly 200 hand-written pages, some of them containing details down to the topography of his grandfather's estate, with its gentle slopes and different types of grass. His description of the interior of the "old barn," his grandfather's house, included the view through the 20-foot-high glass exterior wall of the master bedroom.

Although I had a vested interest, I found myself looking forward to his letters, and greedily reading each one. I did, however, think that he exaggerated parts of his story, especially those of his criminal exploits. In one letter, he wrote that he had put together a sort of mini-mafia, an organization that dealt in extortion and selling guns on a black market, and that state police had formed a task force to capture him. I haven't any proof one way or the other of his claims, and for all I know, they might be true. They just didn't ring that way to me. But I thought that other parts of his story, like his feelings for Jayda and his girlfriend, Jennifer, were honest and told tenderly. "I once enjoyed the company of both my true loves," he wrote about them.

The self-portrait he assembled was both endearing and impressive. I learned that he had a passion for camping and backpacking. I found out that he would "disappear" into the White Mountains in New Hampshire for a week or two with just what he had in his backpack. "The rest," he mentioned, "is found and foraged from nature." He told me that he liked to jump off of waterfalls.

His letters offered glimpses into his dreams. For instance, he mentioned that he's always wanted to sail around the world, "just take a couple of years and sail away."

He wrote at length of his appreciation of literature and his appetite to acquire knowledge. In one letter he listed his favorite scientists and philosophers, among them René Descartes, Ludwig Wittgenstein, Immanuel Kant, Thorstein Veblen, Isaac Newton, and Albert Einstein. "I wish I could one day achieve their levels of intense concentration," he wrote.

From reading his letters, I learned about the Fred Astaire and Ginger Rogers movies he'd watched as a kid. He told me of his love of art, and that his favorite artist was Rembrandt, "followed by Monet." He mentioned that his favorite colors were "the calmness of royal blue, the richness of a dark purple, and the purity of a creamy full yellow."

From his letters, I found out that he pulled out chairs and opened doors for women. He told me that he hated fake and shallow people, although he admitted that "he was known to play the courtier." He mentioned that his favorite flower was the lady's-slipper and that his favorite concert had featured Jethro Tull.

Although my requests were asked in the interest of material for this book, in one instance I inquired, if he could change his future, what would that dream look like?

"Well I took your advice," he wrote back, "and put a dream to paper." Enclosed in the envelope were two pencil drawings. One was a meticulously sketched expansive Colonial home, complete with a columned porch, brick fireplaces and a drive covered with a canopy of winter-bare trees and lined on both sides with a plank-and-post wooden fence. One side of the fence was shaded, as if by an afternoon sun.

And "for comparison," he wrote, he put his reality to paper as well. The second sheet contained a precise pencil drawing of his stark 8 foot–by–10 foot prison cell.

For my first visit at MacDougall–Walker, I was given an hour-and-a-half. Although I'd intended to ask many questions— follow-ups and clarification of people and events mentioned in his letters—I found myself enjoying the conversation as if there weren't Plexiglas between us, and I wasn't there to report a book. Joshua seemed to like our talks too. But he spends twenty-three-and-a-half hours of his day in solitary confinement and has little opportunity for conversation. In fact, at the time of this writing he was no longer allowed visitors—a punishment that perhaps was partly my fault. The Connecticut Department of Correction found out that a writer was visiting Joshua, and not only removed my name from the approved list, but all the names on the list including his parents.

But before I was taken off the list, I visited Joshua three other times, and I would imagine that I knew, outside of his family and a few close friends, more of the full story of

Joshua's life than most. I also knew as much as anyone of his version of the events of July 23, 2007, in Cheshire.

Joshua contends that he didn't kill anyone that morning. He told me that he watched Hayes strangle Mrs. Petit and that, though he wanted to come to her aid, he inexplicably "froze up." He told me that he had taken the pictures of Michaela to blackmail Dr. Petit later on, and insisted that, without her pajamas on, Michaela certainly didn't look 11. But, he didn't, or couldn't, explain the gasoline.

As I walked from the prison after my first visit, I found myself searching for excuses for Joshua's actions. The sexual trauma of his childhood and his parents' refusal to allow him anti-depressants were the first to come to mind. In those moments outside the jail, I wanted to believe that Joshua was also a victim, that there was a fated, tragic element to his life. If only someone had interceded, I thought, and found for him the right therapy and medication, things most certainly would have turned out differently. How could someone who was so tender in writing about his love for his own daughter, be so sympathetic to the poor little girl in Trinidad, I asked myself, not have goodness in his heart? When he had talked to me of the Petit women, he did so with remorse and respect. Most of the time he referred to Jennifer Petit as "Mrs. Petit," except one time when he made the Freudian slip and called her "my mom." He told me he would "gladly exchange his life for those of Jennifer, Hayley and Michaela's."

Maybe it was the thought of Michaela's name coming from Joshua's lips that that brought me back to the reality of why he was then sitting behind Plexiglas and in a prison jumpsuit.

Instead of driving straight towards New York City where I live, I took Route 84 and then the exit for Plainville, the town from which Dr. Petit's family comes, where his practice is, and where his wife and children are buried.

The West Cemetery lies on the side of a gentle slope. The headstones date back to the early 1800s and even before. It's a rather small cemetery and the grounds are dotted with trees, including a towering oak that stands right in the middle and shades most of the grounds. I pulled my car onto the path that led to the bottom of the hill.

The Petits' graves are at the very back edge of the cemetery, just before the tree line of a large wooded area. Almost a year after they were buried, there were still no headstones. Instead, little wooden crosses with bows and pictures of Mrs. Petit, Hayley and Michaela mark their plots.

I stood over them for some time, staring at Michaela's picture. I tried to imagine her asleep next to her mother as Joshua walked into their bedroom. I tried to imagine her expression of confusion and fear when he stripped off her pajamas. I tried to, but couldn't, imagine the terror her expression must have held as the smoke enveloped her room.

As I stood over Michaela's grave I again heard Joshua's soft-spoken voice, I again read his earnest prose, but now his words came as I looked at the smiling face of Michaela on her makeshift grave marker.

The evening sky became as dark as night. I could see nearby streaks of lightning, white rips in the black clouds. I remembered then reading about the funeral procession that made its way from Plainville to Cheshire and back again. As the hearse and cars turned into West Cemetery, Connecticut neighbors with misty eyes lined the route. "We are very much aware that our grief is shared by many of you," a Petit family statement read, "and we are thankful for your prayers and support." But it was Jennifer Hawke-Petit's father, Reverend Richard Hawke, who answered the question that gnawed at this grieving army: Why did God allow this tragedy to occur?

He didn't, the reverend assured them.

"God is crying with us," he said.

Thunder rumbled over the cemetery. Then the rain fell on me in heavy drops. When one friend of Joshua's agreed to talk with me for this book, he did so with a proviso. He asked that I consider Joshua's story as one with the possibility of redemption. If there is redemption in Joshua's future, it is likely that it will come in either a jail cell or on a gurney as he awaits lethal injection. Maybe that day will come. The old adage goes: there are two sides to every story, even one where the good and bad seem so cleary defined as this one. But as I looked down on Michaela's grave, soaked in a rain that fell like tears, I knew that my version of Joshua's story ended right where I stood. No amount of words can excuse his actions.

The letters from Joshua stopped after I was taken off his visitor's list and I haven't written to him since. A few months after my last visit he was transferred out of MacDougall–Walker to Northern Correctional, the prison where Steven Hayes had been held before he was moved to another jail. The wheels of justice in Connecticut grind at an excruciatingly slow pace. As of this writing, nearly two years after that rainy July morning in Cheshire, his trial date has not yet been set.

EPILOGUE

On any summer day, far above Route 84, which climbs through south-central Connecticut, hawks wheel in the white sky. Perhaps now, only after the murders of that July morning in this bedroom community of Cheshire, Connecticut, does the appearance of the majestic birds seem ominous. The flight of the hawks is a reference, of course, to the most famous true crime story, that of a half century and more ago in Holcomb, Kansas.

I don't dare pretend that the previous pages approach the literary perch of Truman Capote's classic. Not by a long shot. But there are undeniable parallels in the two stories: a home invasion, members of a family terrorized and two mismatched ex-cons accused of the murders. They are similar also in the scar these two horrible events left on their communities. In the weeks and months, indeed years, after that rainy morning of July 23, 2007, Cheshire remained a wounded town.

The murders in Cheshire made news around the world. "When Horror Came to a Connecticut Family," screamed *The New York Times*; "Doctor Escapes Attackers Who Killed Family and Set House Ablaze," shouted the London *Times*. Word of the murders reached as far as Ireland and Australia. But in no other place were the emotions as raw as they were in this mostly reserved and gentle New England state. "I don't think there has been a more horrendous murder in the state of Connecticut in the last thirty years," Waterbury State's Attorney John Connelly told *The New York Times*. In an August 8 column in the *New Haven Register*, Randall Beach wrote, "It feels as if this crime is our own '9/11.' The terrorist attacks and the Cheshire murders jolted us into the sudden realization that our world is much crueler, savage and dangerous than we had thought, that we are not as safe as we had believed we were."

In the wake of the murders, some Connecticut folk rushed to arm and alarm, or at least local news stories would have you believe. "I had fifteen calls on my phone by nine thirty in the morning," one Connecticut gun shop owner told a local reporter. "Our phones went absolutely bonkers—we've been very, very busy," James Campochiaro, the owner of Maximum Sound & Security in Southington told *The New York Times*. "People are shaken up by this. They're talking about buying dogs, guns, anything to protect them from an intrusion like this."

Trying to capitalize on the community's fear, ADT Security Services, Inc., a national home alarm company, spread leaflets in Cheshire neighborhoods right after the murders. Angry homeowners complained to the Connecticut Department of Consumer Protection. "I was outraged," said the agency's commissioner on the conduct of the company.

Though fear and outrage were pervasive throughout Connecticut, by no means were they the only reaction to the murders. In blogs and other forums, a few questioned the role of Dr. Petit that morning, wondering why he had been the only one to make it out of the burning home alive. But Dr. Petit's appearance at the memorial services quickly put an end to all such misplaced speculation.

The first service was held in Plainville, the town in which

Dr. Petit had grown up, and where he'd run a private medical practice for many years. Hundreds of friends, acquaintances and patients of the doctor's, known here as "Dr. Billy," gathered on Whiting Street in front of his office. They held candles. Dr. Petit's father, William Petit, Sr., told the crowd that his family must endure. "We have other grandchildren," he said according to *The New York Times*. "We need to go on and be strong for them." Dr. Petit said only a few words, mostly giving thanks for the community's support. He had just been released from St. Mary's Hospital, and he thanked the doctors and staff of that facility. As the candles flickered and began to die away, the doctor, hunch-shouldered, walked through a crowd of weeping townspeople.

But if the Plainville memorial was intimate in its grief, a gathering of high school friends and long-time patients, the service at Central Connecticut State University's gym was an overwhelming expression of outrage and sorrow. The torture, rape and murders of the Petit family had so frightened, so moved Connecticut that the memorial service might have filled a venue twice the size of the college gym—two thousand people or more attended, reports estimated. The nearby student center overflowed with those who couldn't get into the service.

Emotions overflowed too. The stereotypical placid exteriors of soccer moms and executive dads were cracked in tears. Somehow though, the doctor's words allayed the anger. Bruised and wearing an expression that fell somewhere between shock and denial, the doctor stood on a stage next to three large pictures of his dead wife and two daughters. One newspaper report called Dr. Petit's talk "funny, sweet and calm and well-mannered." His humor was self-deprecating, calling himself "a cheap date," when he recounted meeting his future wife in the Pittsburgh hospital.

Though his family was gone, he was still a father, one filled with pride and love when he talked about his daughters. He told of how he'd warned Michaela, "K.K.," as he called her, that she'd have to learn how to do her homework in the car as Hayley had on their way to the University of Connecticut basketball games. Even when he alluded to the murders, he was able to find hope. "If any good is going to come of this," he said, "it's going to have to come from you. It's going to have come from all of us," he said to the audience.

But in still another memorial, some months later, he seemed to lose whatever grace was allowing him to endure. A reporter from the *New Haven Register* witnessed Dr. Petit's human frailty at the end of that memorial: "Only when he had finished speaking and turned to leave did the microphone capture terrible gasps that escaped from his lungs," the reporter wrote. "They were the sound of grief in an endless void."

The police response to the incident on Sorghum Mill Drive came under intense scrutiny. The Cheshire Police Department went into bunker mentality as reporters and bloggers questioned the actions—or lack thereof—the morning of July 23. "The Cheshire Police Department's officers acted properly and according to their training," said the Cheshire Police Department spokesman, Lieutenant Jay Markella.

Cheshire Town Manager Michael Milone went as far as *praising* the way his department had handled the crime: "Without their great work this could have been a far worse tragedy," he said. It's hard to imagine how much worse it could have gotten. Twenty minutes at least passed between the time when the first Cheshire cop was on foot and nearing the Petits' backyard and when the Pacifica crashed into the police barricade. Neighbors heard screams coming from the

Petit home while cops were setting up perimeters. Michaela or Hayley or both were alive while Cheshire police were in their backyard following procedure.

On the first anniversary of the murders, Jennifer Hawke-Petit's parents, the Reverend Richard and Marybelle Hawke, broke their silence in the press with a scathing assessment of the police response that morning. A letter they wrote to the prosecutor and shared with the Associated Press read in part:

> We indeed are victims of the silence and we have been very disturbed with the untruthfulness to protect the negligence of action to intervene in this home invasion. That could have stopped the murders.

The Hawkes' sentiments echoed blog entries that called the Cheshire police "Keystone Kops," and "Barney Fife."

The harshness of the cyberspace assessment is unfair—no one could have imagined what was transpiring within the Petits' home, and most police work follows a book that is not authored by a Hollywood scriptwriter. One thing is for certain, however: there were no heroes outside the Petit home that morning.

"In Cheshire, we're not used to this type of event," said Cheshire Police Chief Michael Cruess.

Perhaps the only person alive who could let the cops off the hook, did. With his enduring grace, Dr. Petit publicly thanked the Cheshire Police Department for their help.

But if Dr. Petit's words exonerated the cops, another arm of Connecticut's criminal justice system was not so lucky. Four months after his family was murdered, Dr. Petit sent an email, time-stamped at 1:50 a.m., to a neighbor who is also a

Connecticut State Representative. Alfred Adinolfi read the message to the Connecticut State Legislature's Judiciary Committee:

> Those horrible events not only took the lives of my beautiful and wonderful wife and daughters, but they also exposed some glaring defects in our laws and their inability to adequately ensure our public safety. Every resident of Connecticut deserves to have those glaring deficiencies in our public safety laws corrected.

Politically charged, the weeks and months after the Cheshire murders saw a public cry for change, especially in the process of parole. Connecticut's governor, M. Jodi Rell, ordered a "top to bottom" review of her state's criminal justice system. Steven Hayes's release had never been satisfactorily explained. Joshua was granted parole release without the parole board reviewing his sentencing transcript (required by law). It was in that transcript where Judge Bentivegna called Joshua a "cold, calculating predator," where Joshua's own lawyer said that, by all rights, his client could be sentenced to 30 years, and where Ronald Dearstyne said that he hadn't seen a criminal the likes of Joshua in his fifteen years as a prosecutor. Later it was revealed that often parole boards don't receive documents such as the transcript because of the cost of the copies and the time it takes to make them.

Governor Rell responded to the outcry by slapping a moratorium on felony parole, stretching the physical limits of the jails. Rell also ordered the release of Joshua's and Hayes's parole records to the press, nearly 500 pages that formed a sweeping indictment of Connecticut's parole system. The documents showed how statements like the one Connecticut's supervisory state's attorney had made that Steven Hayes had "virtually no history of violence" were ludicrous on the surface and patently false in substance.

In July of 2007, just after the Cheshire murders, Governor Rell announced new parole standards for nighttime burglars. "Burglary has long been considered a generally non-violent offense, but those who commit these crimes at night or when a home is occupied are far more likely to encounter a homeowner—meaning the chances of violence are increased exponentially," she said in a press release.

The governor also ordered GPS monitoring systems for parolees and unannounced visits at night and at workplaces by parole officers. She also asked the state's legislature to move to reclassify Burglary II as a violent offense. In Connecticut, violent offenders must serve 85 percent of their sentences. Joshua was released after serving only 50 percent. "Security comes first," Rell said in a September 21 statement. "I will not allow public safety to be jeopardized because parolees return to a life of crime. Parole is a privilege, not a right."

Seven months after the Cheshire murders, Governor Rell praised legislative leaders and the members of the judiciary committee for working in a bipartisan fashion to develop the criminal justice reform package for her state, which passed 36–0 in the Senate and 126–12 in the House. The bill made home invasion a violent crime.

But the governor's hard line of reform began to show cracks before it was even implemented. One of the provisions was to revise the parole board to include full-time positions and state-of-the-art information sharing. On the eve of the confirmation hearings for the new parole board positions, the names of two nominees were abruptly withdrawn. Members of the part-time parole board for years, those two men had served on at least one of the panels that reviewed Joshua Komisar-jevsky's case. Governor Rell defended her choices as former decorated police officers. Her office was aware, she said, of the two men having served on Joshua's parole hearing, a statement that brought a concerned reaction from her constituency and the ire of her political rivals. "The case is particularly emblematic of a systemic collapse," said state senate judiciary committee's co-chairman, Andrew McDonald, a Democrat from Stamford.

For the extended Petit family, the political infighting mattered little, and the reforms came years too late to save their loved ones.

In the wake of the murders, there was a considerable amount of bloodlust, especially in the blogosphere. Post after post called for punishments far worse than anything the government allows. As it happened, at the same time Joshua and Hayes were being arraigned on capital felony murder charges that could bring a sentence of death by lethal injection, the highest court in the land was debating the constitutionality of that form of execution.

The debate over the inhumanity of lethal injection goes all the way back to the late 1800s. Then the medical community won out, and injection as a way of executing the condemned was shelved for many years. Nazi Germany used lethal injection in Auschwitz and other concentration camps, but gas proved much more convenient. In 1977, the very public execution by firing squad of Gary Gilmore, an event that dominated headlines for months and inspired Norman Mailer to write a Pulitzer Prize–winning novel, reenergized the anti-death penalty movement. With the necessity of a low-profile and low-cost method of execution, the chief medical examiner of Oklahoma, Dr. Jay Chapman, invented a "three-drug cocktail" as a means of execution. Oklahoma state legislators ratified the method and thirty-six other states including Connecticut followed their example.

Chapman's method works like this: The execution team inserts an IV line, and then the condemned is given sodium pentothal, the first of three drugs. Sodium pentothal, classified as an "ultrashort-acting barbiturate," is meant to render the inmate deeply unconscious within ninety seconds. A second drug, pancuronium bromide, a muscle relaxant that paralyzes all skeletal muscles, including the diaphragm, inhibits the condemned from gasping, moaning or flopping around on the gurney, and possibly disturbing witnesses of the execution. The third drug, concentrated potassium chloride, stops the heart.

The method isn't exactly foolproof.

The first execution by lethal injection was in Texas in 1982. Charles Brooks, Jr., was condemned to death for killing a garage mechanic. Instead of following the protocol set up by Chapman, the warden mixed all three ingredients together, forming a thick paste that was put into a syringe. When a doctor examined him to certify death, he found Brooks still breathing.

In the recent past, "execution teams" throughout prisons in the United States were rarely trained. In 2006, a man who was being executed in Ohio raised his head during the procedure and said, "It's not working." In Florida in 2006, Angel Diaz took a half hour to die from the cocktail. His corpse had foot-long chemical burns on both arms.

But regardless of the many mishaps, death penalty proponents have examples where the punishment, they say, fits the crime. In 1994, the United States Supreme Court denied a review of the death penalty case of *Callins* v. *Collins*. In a rebuttal during that case, Justice Antonin Scalia wrote:

. . . for example, the case of the 11-year-old girl raped
by four men and then killed by stuffing her panties
down her throat. See *McCollum* v. *North Carolina* . . .
How enviable a quiet death by lethal injection compared with that!

In 2007, the United States Supreme Court imposed a moratorium on executions while it ruled on whether or not Chapman's three-drug cocktail constituted cruel and unusual
punishment, protection from which is guaranteed by the
Eighth Amendment. In April of 2008, the court ruled 7–2
that Kentucky's method of executing prisoners by lethal injection was not in violation of the amendment, which allowed execution as an option in the Petit murder trial.
    Though the Supreme Court would rule in favor of lethal
injection, the debate lived on in another court, one with a
jurisdiction that was at once far more encompassing than
that ruled by laws of man, and also one as close to the Petit
home as a leisurely Sunday drive.

The United Methodist Church of which Jennifer Hawke-Petit
and her family were prominent members has for a generation
or two aligned itself against capital punishment. And, according to an article in *The New York Times*, Jennifer Petit had
signed a document called "A Declaration of Life" that was en-
dorsed by members of her church. The document reads in part:

    I, the undersigned, being of sound and disposing mind
    and memory, do hereby in the presence of witnesses
    make this Declaration of Life.
    I believe that the killing of one human being by an-
    other is morally wrong.

I believe it is morally wrong for any state or other governmental entity to take the life of a human being for any reason.

I believe that capital punishment is not a deterrent to crime and serves only the purpose of revenge.

THEREFORE, I hereby declare that should I die as a result of a violent crime, I request that the person or persons found guilty of homicide for my killing not be subject to or put in jeopardy of the death penalty under any circumstances, no matter how heinous their crime or how much I may have suffered. The death penalty would only increase my suffering.

According to the *Times* article, at least two members of the church witnessed Jennifer Petit signing the document. Carolyn Hardin Engelhardt, a church member who is also the director of the ministry resource center at Yale Divinity School Library, told the *Times* reporter, "It'd be so dishonoring to her life to do anything violent in her name. That's not the kind of person she was."

But a blog titled "Rhymes with Right" had this to say about the signing of that document:

. . . the views of Jennifer Hawke-Petit (or her daughters, or her surviving husband and other family members) on the death penalty are at best tangentially relevant to the eventual sentence given in this case. When prosecuted, the case will not be prosecuted in her name—it will be prosecuted in the name of the people of the state of Connecticut, recognizing that the offense committed was not just against her and her family, but also against society as a whole.

Connecticut has put only one person to death since 1960. On May 13, 2005, Michael Ross, a convicted serial killer, received a lethal injection. One hundred protestors, including members of the United Methodist Church in Cheshire, and Thomas Ullman, New Haven Public Defender and Steven Hayes's attorney, gathered in protest outside the prison walls.

Hayes's attorney is one of the state of Connecticut's foremost opponents of the death penalty, and may be the most experienced in fighting it in court. His courtroom persona has been called "passionate" in published reports. He is also known to use unusual strategies in trying to spare the lives of those clients accused of capital crimes. In 2000, he represented Jonathan Mills, who was charged with slashing to death a 43-year-old woman and her two small children. The prosecutor, Michael Dearington, who is also representing the state in the Cheshire murders, sought the death penalty for Mills. After his client was convicted, Ullman was able to persuade a judge to allow Mills to speak directly to the jury—a very rare tactic. Mills's remorseful apology saved his life, as the jury voted against putting him to death.

Joshua has also been assigned a high-profile attorney. Jeremiah Donovan from Old Saybrook, Connecticut, has had trial closing arguments reprinted in several law reviews as examples of "cinematic storytelling." No stranger to newsprint, Donovan has represented clients who have made headlines, including Heather Specyalski who Donovan successfully represented with what would become known as "the Lewinsky defense." Specyalski was charged with manslaughter in the death of her boyfriend, a wealthy businessman who was killed in a drunk driving accident. Though the prosecution contended that Specyalski, who couldn't remember details after the accident, was driving the car, Donovan argued that his client couldn't have been driving because she

was in the passenger seat performing a sex act on her boyfriend. The businessman's body was found partially clad at
the accident scene. The jury agreed with Donovan and ac-
quitted Specyalski.

As for representing Joshua, Donovan promised to "pour
all his efforts into blocking the death penalty."

In all, 102 people have been executed in Connecticut in
the state's history. According to the Connecticut Department
of Correction website, there are at this writing ten inmates on
Connecticut's death row, Northern Correctional Institution in
Somers, Connecticut. Perhaps two more will be added in the
coming months.

After his arrest in Cheshire, Steven Hayes was sent to a
segregated unit in Northern Correctional. With a reputation
of holding the worst of Connecticut's criminals, any length
of time served at Northern is hard. Time waiting to die there
is incomprehensible. The unit in which Hayes is confined is
made up of two blocks of twenty-five solid-wall cells. Witnesses to his plight have said that Hayes has lost a considerable amount of weight; his prison jumpsuit hangs from the
frame. He is only allowed to shave in the presence of a corrections officer, but most of the time he doesn't bother, giving him a scraggly, even deranged appearance. His recreation
time is one half hour each day, but he hardly ever leaves the
cell. One reason is that he fears for his personal safety. Governor Rell's mandate revoked parole for many inmates from
the nearby Enfield Correctional Institution. Regularly Enfield
inmates are transported to Northern for prison maintenance
and other details. If Hayes ever found himself in a quiet corner with a con whose parole had been revoked "they'd kill
him," said one corrections officer from Northern. But another reason Hayes doesn't leave the cell is that his only
visitors are his lawyers. In late 2008, Hayes was transferred

to Garner Correctional Institution in Newtown, Connecticut, where he is on a one-on-one, round-the-clock suicide watch.

As both Joshua and Steven Hayes await their fate, a debate over capital punishment in Connecticut continues. In June of 2009, the state's legislature passed a bill that sought to abolish the death penalty. Governor Rell vetoed the legislation. A recent poll indicated that a majority of Connecticut voters were in favor of the death penalty. Undoubtedly, the ominous shadow of the Cheshire murders had a great influence on that poll and the governor's decision. The heart of the argument for the death penalty is that it is a deterrent. That heart beats quickly in Connecticut, especially in homes where the thought of what happened in Cheshire is no longer unimaginable.